MIDNIGHT IN THE AMERICAN EMPIRE

HOW CORPORATIONS AND THEIR POLITICAL SERVANTS ARE DESTROYING THE AMERICAN DREAM

ROBERT BRIDGE

ISBN: 1480209465
ISBN-13: 9781480209466
Library of Congress Control Number: 2012920558
CreateSpace Independent Publishing Platform
North Charleston, South Carolina

CONTENTS

Preface

We the American people are now confronting the ultimate threat: Despite our fierce devotion to independence and freedom, a handful of powerful, interconnected corporations provide for all of our social and cultural needs. They feed us, dress us, and lend us a mortgage. They deliver news and entertainment into our living rooms 24/7. When the pain and suffering is too great, they sell us the costly medication. Since most entrepreneurial opportunities have been consumed by these monolithic monsters, we depend upon corporations to provide us with jobs and a decent retirement. In short, we depend on corporations for everything. The American Dream, however, will never be found on a shelf at Wal-Mart. The tragic irony of our predicament is that at the same time that corporations provide us with everything, they take away what is most precious: our freedom, liberty and democracy.

Today, the primary goal of corporate America is no longer the age-old task of making money. Its goal is to control the economic, social, and political realms, and that task is nearly accomplished. In direct opposition to the spirit of the US Constitution, this usurper has purchased a commanding presence inside our dual-party political system, yet it is not held accountable by democratic due process. From the recent passage of fiercely pro-business legislation, to a well-funded lobbying and campaign-funding apparatus, our government representatives have become the submissive servants of corporate interests. Like a quickly spreading cancer, unchecked corporate power is inflicting irreparable damage to the political body; it must be removed before the republic suffers total collapse. Yet, we close our eyes to our situation in the belief that corporations and the people who manage them are somehow a complement to democratic procedure. They are not.

Meanwhile, as corporate entities become the new star players inside our communities, we the people — the rugged individuals who made America great — can only watch passively from the sidelines. This dramatic role reversal has been forced upon us by a number of stunning court decisions that have awarded corporations "personhood," while allowing them to avoid the unpleasantries that come with such a designation (like politely dying, paying their fair share of the tax load, and remaining outside the political arena, for example). This corporate hijacking was made possible by the unconstitutional collaboration between the corporate and political worlds.

From Main Street to Wall Street, however, people are starting to ask some hard questions concerning this unprecedented power grab. For example, where do the boundaries of civil society and the corporate world begin and end? What are the consequences for our democratic heritage if there are no definite boundaries separating the political realm from the economic? What does this radical transformation mean for our political system, which is largely dominated by two parties, both of which receive the lion's share of their campaign funding from the corporate world? Should the business world be separated from politics, as was the case with the separation of church and state? Finally, what does the growth of corporate power mean for our "rugged individualism," which grants individual men and women the right to compete against their fellow men (as capitalism originally intended) as opposed to behemoth and faceless organizations?

The regularly upbeat world of big business, long before the financial crisis of 2008 exploded on the scene, was beginning to express similar concerns over what is becoming the primary issue of our times. "Old certainties," wrote the *Financial Times* in a candid May Day editorial, "have been replaced by a vision of a lawless world beyond individuals' control, in which profit-seeking corporations trample freely over local cultures. While few people seem prepared to sacrifice capitalism's advantages, many yearn somehow to put up the shutters."[1]

Even the maestro of economics himself, Alan Greenspan, who served for almost two decades as the chairman of the Federal Reserve Board, admitted that despite the elimination of communism as a rival, capitalism and globalization are also not out of the woods. "While central planning may no longer be a credible form of economic organization, it is clear that the intellectual battle for its rival—free-market capitalism and globalization—is far from won," he wrote. Then, after providing a litany of capitalism's greatest achievements, such as reducing poverty and increasing life expectancy, Greenspan admitted that for many, "Capitalism still seems difficult to accept, much less fully embrace."[2]

According to a recent poll, faith in the free market has hit an all-time low in the United States. In 2002, 80 percent of Americans interviewed by GlobeScan, a polling agency, agreed "strongly" or "somewhat" that the free market was the best economic system for organizing our society. By 2010, the number of individuals who reported unshakable faith in unfettered markets dropped to 59 percent of the respondents. Among the less privileged strata of Americans, those earning under $20,000, "faith in capitalism fell from 76% to 44% in just one year."[3]

When properly tuned, corporate capitalism is the motor that drives some of mankind's greatest achievements. When it falls out of sync, however, it is the most dangerous economic system ever conceived, and certainly the most vulnerable to public backlash. Indeed, in light of the grassroots movement against globalization, many people sense that this great experiment is hanging by the end of its spiritual and physical rope. Such sentiments have only been exasperated with the 2008 economic meltdown, which witnessed

---

1   *Financial Times*, May 1, 2001, 12.

2   Alan Greenspan, *The Age of Turbulence* (London: Penguin Books, 2008), 267–268.

3   "Market troubles," *The Economist*, April 6, 2011. For GlobeScan data, see http://www.globescan.com/news_archives/radar10w2_free_market/).

the culprits of that global crisis, namely, the financial institutions and transnational corporations, escape largely unscathed thanks to a massive government bailout and buy-in. This robbery in broad daylight has led to breathless levels of economic, social, and political inequality that can no longer be ignored.

Today, the economists, corporations, and financial institutions are calling the shots inside our democracy, and this has had a significant impact on other areas of life not directly related to business. The corporate agenda has no respect for the more sensitive areas of life, such as culture, philosophy, and the environment. Therefore, it is necessary to address subjects outside the immediate realm of economics that are extremely vulnerable to invasions by concentrated forces of economic power. The specter of corporate power influencing every aspect of our lives—from the types of programs our children are watching on television, to the extent that corporations sponsor our presidential campaigns, to even the way we wage war—goes to the very heart of our national heritage. Indeed, it goes to the heart of what it means to be American.

Corporate power has achieved a degree of influence in our daily lives that would have been condemned as absolutely scandalous by our Founding Fathers. Thus, it is our patriotic duty to decide whether the current level of corporate power and influence is destructive to the republic in the long run. If we arrive at the conclusion that it is, then now is the time to act. The decisions we make (or fail to make) at this critical historic juncture will forever affect the course of our nation's destiny.

Today, more than ever before, the great debate on globalization demands an input of fresh voices. After all, it is not just the economists, bankers, and politicians who have a stake in this great transformation of American life. And unlike the many academics and statesmen who have never had the pleasure of working inside the very system they passionately advocate, many of us, including the author, have experienced globalization firsthand from inside the belly of the corporate beast. During my lengthy relationship with the corporate world, I came to the realization that something is conspicuously missing inside this system. That something, I believe, is nothing less than democracy.

Business leaders regularly trumpet the virtues of the "free market," while at the same time ignoring how individuals are treated inside this "free" system. As the road to happiness becomes increasingly privatized in the hands of a few powerful individuals and their untouchable organizations, we risk reaching a point of no return when the people, finally understanding that their voice cannot match that of the corporate overlords, will take to other less salubrious means of exacting justice. Needless to say, such a destructive course of action must be avoided at all cost. In the absence of some form of "corporate democracy" to defend ourselves against infinitely powerful organizations, no political party can hope to address these many grievances. The issues are supranational and require a whole new modus operandi.

Finally, this book asks a simple question that has no simple answer: How can we as citizens and consumers of a capitalist democracy address the unprecedented cultural, social, and political changes that globalization in general and corporations in particular have forced upon us? It is taken for granted that change, in all of its various costumes, is an inescapable part of modern life and, for the most part, a positive thing. Thus, we silently acquiesce to the radical new rules of the global game: stable jobs with decent benefits are an increasing rarity, retraining to keep pace with the technological changes is an endless requirement, while our local communities have turned into stomping grounds for transnational corporations. At the very same time that we are expected to accept the radical makeover of our nation, we have surrendered our political voice to the corporate world. This situation, which is devoid of even the faintest notion of democracy, is unacceptable.

Before the social pendulum swings back in less-than-rational reaction to what has become corporate malfeasance on the grandest level, we must return the American rugged individual back to his due place in the natural order of things, and that is as the leading figure inside his many diverse neighborhoods and communities. Corporations may be many things that the legal system wants them to be, but they will never substitute for the human individual.

April 3, 2012

CHAPTER I
Taking Care of Business (As Usual)

In the real world, the autonomous individual is not the active agent who matters most. The business enterprise, the company, the corporation is. And companies do everything they can to take advantage of human changeability.

—JAMES K. GALBRAITH, *THE PREDATOR STATE*

We the American people, whose creation story began many years ago with a struggle against kings, queens, and oppressive regimes, believe that the road to happiness should be equally accessible to all who wish to travel upon it. Irrespective of an individual's inherited status or condition, the Founding Fathers bequeathed to all Americans a level playing field. This was their most enduring gift to every citizen, and it explains why our nation was forged in the fires of revolution: Great things are rarely acquired without an epic struggle. Today, however, we have taken the priceless gift of our ancestors for granted. We have betrayed the work of America's founders by failing to defend the inheritance of freedom and liberty in the face of arbitrary economic powers.

Today, the only things necessary for achieving the American Dream, we believe, are dedication to good old-fashioned initiative, perseverance, and self-sacrifice. Every individual has the power to pull through the darkest hour through sheer will and determination. This unshakable faith in the power of the individual, however, fails to appreciate the new realities that have taken the world by storm. Neighborhoods big and small are forced to reckon with veritable global empires, the transnational corporations, which in many cases possess greater wealth and influence than sovereign states. This new economic paradigm has opened the door to insurmountable challenges that transcend purely business interests. Indeed, economic "special interests" have practically usurped the US political process.

One manifestation of this travesty is that corporations have "legally" acquired all of the constitutional powers once reserved explicitly for the American people. In legal jargon, corporations have acquired "personhood." This extreme interpretation of the Constitution has led to an unprecedented transferral of power, influence, and wealth into the hands of a minute minority of the population known to the Occupy Wall Street movement as the "1 percent." Given the disproportionate influence of these individuals and the political powers they have purchased, we are witnessing the rise of an American aristocracy anchored on corporate power in the very land that fought a revolution to free itself from the yoke of entitlement and privilege.

Before we continue, it must be admitted that the elite are a vital force for any culture worthy of the name; they provide the brains and the economic support that keep society on the road of progress. Their financial clout bankrolls civilization's greatest achievements. Their resources finance the discovery of breakthrough technologies, which in turn drives the economy. In other words, the hierarchical ranking of individuals according to their inherent capabilities or inherited status is arguably an inevitable social process. Even the communists were forced to break with the teachings of Karl Marx and create their own "revolutionary" vanguard of pampered elites known as the Communist Party, a mighty minority at the top of the Soviet hierarchy that never had to wait in bread lines. The philosopher Bertrand Russell summed up this great paradox when he spoke a terrible truth: "To some extent, civilization is furthered by social injustice."[4]

Although the elite play a crucial role in mobilizing society to its fullest potential, these individuals, at the same time, rarely lead with a moral compass in hand. Their interest is predominantly a self-interest; greed is a human vice not limited to particular social classes or historical periods. Indeed, man is an opportunistic creature, and it is the rare exception when he fails to betray his own brother if the price is right. This was proved by the 2008 global financial crisis, a cataclysmic event triggered by a level of greed, fraud, and deception that will keep the US economy in a straitjacket for many years to come. Now, with many Americans reeling from economic hardship, the onus is on the proponents of globalization to prove that the economic system really is designed with the average person's best interest at heart. This will be capitalism's most difficult sell to date. After all, even the most dedicated proponents admit to capitalism's deep contradictions, which continuously beat against the very foundation of the country.

"Capitalism," noted Peter F. Drucker, one of the leading voices on business management, "is being attacked not because it is inefficient or misgoverned but because it is cynical. And indeed a society based on the assertion that private vices become public benefits cannot endure, no matter how impeccable the logic, no matter how great its benefits."[5] Drucker warned that the endless hostility to capitalism and capitalists is based on "moral and ethical" arguments that wise men would do well to heed.

"The laws of social development," wrote Isaiah Berlin, discussing one possible future for mankind as predicted by Karl Marx, "make it inevitable that at a certain stage of history one class, pursuing its interests with varying degrees of rationality, should dispossess and exploit another, and so lead to the repression and crippling of men."[6] The economist James K. Galbraith described

---

4   Bertrand Russell, *History of Western Philosophy* (London: Routledge Classics, 2004), 579.

5   Peter F. Drucker, *The Practice of Management* (New Delhi: Allied Publishers, 1955), 392.

6   Isaiah Berlin, *Karl Marx* (Oxford University Press, 1996), 5.

the behind-the-scenes greed now cannibalizing the global economy as "rule by predators" in which the rules of the game work to the advantage of "organized business and banking lobbies."[7]

Indeed, the individuals sitting pretty at the commanding heights of the global economy seem to lack the chromosome for moral prudence. When pressed for details—a rare event in itself—they reveal the absurdity of their belief system. Lloyd Blankfein, for example, the chief executive of Goldman Sachs, the investment firm whose shady practices were largely responsible for sparking the 2008 crisis, proclaimed he and his fellow colleagues are simply performing "God's work."[8] Now how is it possible to argue against the behavior of a man who has God in his corner?

In fact, the miraculous hand of God is conspicuous everywhere you look in the American financial system. Certainly the Almighty was whispering advice into the ear of John Thain, the former CEO of Merrill Lynch who aggressively pushed through $3.62 billion in bonus pay for his executives in December 2008 rather than wait until January as was customary. There was a good reason why Thain was anxious to speed up the paperwork. After Merrill Lynch was taken over by Bank of America, it was revealed that the former CEO had lost his company $15.3 million in the fourth quarter of 2008.[9] The work of God did not end there. Just months after JPMorgan Chase lobbyists were in Washington fighting against already weak financial regulatory law, JPMorgan Chase CEO Jamie Dimon announced that his company had lost billions of dollars on risky hedge bets—something that government supervisory powers could have thwarted. Clearly, the rot runs deep, and it is outright blasphemous to mention the name of the Almighty in the same breath as these blatant crimes. Meanwhile, our business leaders, who believe that God is their captain, regularly demand an end to all gov-

7   James K. Galbraith, *The Predator State* (New York: Free Press, 2009), xiv.
8   Helen Coster, "The Biggest CEO Outrages of 2009," *Forbes*, Nov. 25, 2009. Apparently "doing God's work" is reasonable employment considering that the Goldman Sachs' chief earned a cool $73 million in 2007, the same year the global economy imploded. Incidentally, Goldman Sachs, and despite its dubious business practices, donated $994,795 to Barack Obama's presidential election campaign, his largest contributor.
9   Coster, *Forbes.*

ernment regulations. Personal self-enrichment no matter what the cost is the first law of the jungle; the second law says the people must rescue the bankers and investors when the latter get burned by their insatiable greed.

Unscrupulous corporate behavior continues unabated despite, or because of, the most devastating economic storm to hit the US mainland since the Great Depression. And as the killer wave of that economic tsunami slowly recedes, the debris from years of corporate greed and recklessness are being painfully revealed. The golden age of opportunity that our fathers and grandfathers enjoyed, and despite the fact that most American families today are two-income households, is over. The raw data tell a tragic story.

BEFORE AND AFTER THE STORM

Let's admit it: Statistics bore the heck out of us. Mindlessly rattling off reams of economic data is a tedious exercise that has a tendency to backfire and desensitize us to the reality of the situation. Nevertheless, let's be patient for a moment and briefly consider the numbers in order to appreciate the extent of our predicament.

First, the "economic crisis" that began to wash across an unsuspecting planet in late 2007 is just the latest in a series of many economic setbacks to plague the American people. The recent collapse of the global banks and financial markets marked the latest chapter of a tragedy that has been steadily unfolding for many decades. Indeed, no matter how the spin doctors twist US labor data over the past forty years, it is nearly impossible to find a silver lining. As the *Financial Times* summed up the grim reality: "The annual incomes of the bottom 90 percent of US families have been essentially flat since 1973—having risen only by 10 percent in real terms over the past 37 years"—despite the rise in two-income homes.[10] Over the same period, however, the incomes of the top 1 percent have smashed through the roof.

---

10   Edward Luce, "The Crisis of Middle-Class America," *Financial Times*, July 30, 2010.

A study by the Economic Policy Institute[11] showed that chief executives at America's 350 largest companies were paid 231 times as much as the average private-sector worker in 2011 (by comparison, CEOs earned just 20.1 times more than average workers in 1965). It is important to note that this CEO-worker wage ratio peaked around 2000 at 384 times. Although the recession temporarily tamped down income inequality, CEO pay is once again on the rise while worker pay remains stagnant.

The report shows that one of the main reasons for rising inequality in the United States "is the wage gap between the very highest earners—those in the upper 1.0 percent or even upper 0.1 percent—and other earners, including other high-wage earners." The study points to "those at the top" of the corporate pyramid for aggravating the unequal growth in incomes. "The average annual earnings of the top 1 percent of wage earners grew 156 percent from 1979 to 2007; for the top 0.1 percent they grew 362 percent," it said.

For those who have forgotten what the economic climate inside of the United States was like before the 2008 economic tsunami made landfall, consider the following. The *Economist*, quoting Julia Isaacs of the Brookings Institute, reported that "between 1974 and 2004 median wages for men in their 30s, adjusted for inflation, fell by 12% from $40,000 to $35,000." [12] The *Wall Street Journal*, calling this middleclass bloodletting "the lost decade," reported: "The inflation-adjusted income of the median household—smack in the middle of the populace—fell 4.8% between 2000 and 2009, even worse than the 1970s, when median income rose 1.9% despite high unemployment and inflation. Between 2007 and 2009, incomes fell 4.2%." The article provided a candid comment by Nicholas Eberstadt, a political economist at the right-leaning American Enterprise Institute: "It's going to be a long, hard slog back to what most Americans think of as normalcy or prosperous times."[13] That dire prognosis may eventually prove to

11   Lawrence Mishel and Natalie Sabadish, "CEO Pay and the Top 1%," Economic Policy Institute, May 2, 2012.

12   Lexington, "Down, but Not Necessarily Out," *Economist*, June 6, 2009, 46.

13   Conor Dougherty and Sara Murray, "Lost Decade for Family Income," *Wall Street Journal*, Sept. 17, 2010.

be overly optimistic since many economists believe the best days of the American economy are gone forever.

Yet another way to understand what is happening in US labor markets is to look at the number of "shared households," which have soared since 2007. According to the US Census Bureau, in 2007 "there were 19.7 million shared households, representing 17.0 percent of all households; by 2012, there were 22.3 million shared households. The number of adults in shared households grew from 61.7 million (27.7 percent) in 2007 to 69.5 million (29.6) in 2012."[14]

The hardest thing to accept about this fantastic reversal of fortune is that much of the present pain and suffering was largely avoidable. It would have required self-restraint, political will, and very little sacrifice, but the bleeding of the American middle class was nothing less than a deliberate, premeditated crime. As the *Financial Times* revealed, "the share of the US income that goes to workers as wages rather than to investors as profits…has fallen to its lowest level since records began after the Second World War."[15] The most reputable business newspaper in the world was forced to admit that "something strange and unprecedented is going on" inside the US economy. Strange, indeed. According to the above-mentioned report, the present economic crisis is a wildly different animal from past recessions and depressions. In past crises, "the labour share tends to rise during recessions as companies hold on to workers and sacrifice profits, then falls back in a recovery," according to *FT.* "But during the 2008 recession the labour share did the opposite: it fell, and when the recovery began it kept falling."

Here comes the bloody kicker: "If wages were at their postwar average share of 63 percent, workers would earn an extra $740bn this year, about $5,000 per worker," the *FT* article reveals. Labor's

---

14   "Income, Poverty, and Health Insurance Coverage in the United States: 2011," US Census Bureau, September, 2012. The report defines a 'shared household' as a household that includes at least one "additional" adult, a person aged 18 years or older who is not enrolled in school and is not the householder spouse, or cohabiting partner of the householder."

15   Robin Harding, "Pay Gap a $740bn Threat to US Recovery," *Financial Times*, December 14, 2011.

slice of the income pie has decreased to 58 percent, a historic low that still has not hit bottom. This unprecedented disparity in wage distribution explains why the US economy is furiously spinning its wheels, while only the corporations seem to be advancing. Meanwhile, labor is always one precarious step away from becoming road kill. "The decline in the US labour share, along with a shift of labour income towards higher earners, may be an important part of why the US economic recovery is so sluggish," the *FT* article concludes. "Instead of hoarding labour and cutting prices to grab market share, companies are sacking workers, holding prices and choosing to buy back their own equity rather than make new investments." Clearly, the corporate executive class is indulging itself to an all-you-can-eat smorgasbord at the salary trough, and with a void of democratic procedure inside the workplace, nobody is forcing them away from the table.

THE EXORBITANT COST OF A "FREE MARKET"

Since the early 1980s, and irrespective of the political party holding court on Pennsylvania Avenue, the US economy has been guided by the principles of the Reagan-Thatcher economic model, which holds to the belief that laissez-faire capitalism is the best system for organizing society. This economic philosophy, however, was known long before Ronald Reagan and Margaret Thatcher stepped onto the political stage. In fact, the man who popularized the idea of laissez-faire economics over two hundred years ago, Adam Smith, would be shocked to see what is passed off today as capitalism and fair competition. The author of *The Wealth of Nations,* published in 1776, has been grossly misrepresented in order to sell a severely damaged product to the people.

"Laissez-faire was intended to establish a world community as well as a natural harmony of interests within each nation," the theologian and social critic Reinhold Niebuhr observed.[16] Smith's

---

16   Reinhold Niebuhr, *The Children of Light and the Children of Darkness* (New York: Charles Scribner's Sons, 1944), 26.

dogma, which was designed to "guarantee the economic freedom of the individual," was grotesquely distorted in order to become the ideology of "vast corporate structures of a later period of capitalism, used by them, and still used, to prevent a proper political control of their power."

According to Niebuhr, corporate interests hijacked an otherwise sound economic philosophy and substituted it with one that is altogether void of morality and political sense. Such conditions, he warned, would naturally lead to class conflicts. "Smith's vision of international harmony was transmuted into the sorry realities of an international capitalism," Niebuhr warned, "which recognized neither moral scruples nor political restraints in expanding its power over the world. His vision of a democratic harmony of society, founded upon the free play of economic forces, was refuted by the tragic realities of the class conflicts of Western society."

Meanwhile, with no loss of irony, the proponents of laissez-faire demand that government stay out of the boardroom, while, at the same time, never too far away in case of an emergency; a classic example of having your economy and eating it too. Yet corporate America's demand for less government interference and regulation is what led to the downfall of our economy in the first place. So how did our fearless leaders punish the corporate executives for dragging the global economy to the abyss? By turning on the printing presses and handing them billions of dollars, courtesy of the Federal Reserve. According to 29,000 pages of Fed documents obtained under the Freedom of Information Act and central bank records of more than 21,000 transactions, "the Fed had committed $7.77 trillion as of March 2009 to rescuing the financial system, more than half the value of everything produced in the United States that year."[17] The article then provides the following statement, which should raise serious alarm: "While Fed officials say that almost all of the loans were repaid and there have been no losses, *details suggest taxpayers paid a price beyond dollars as the secret funding helped preserve a broken status quo and enabled*

---

17   Bob Ivry, Bradley Keoun and Phil Kuntz, "Secret Fund Loans Gave Banks $13 Billion Undisclosed to Congress," Bloomberg Markets Magazine, November 27, 2011.(italics added).

the biggest banks to grow even bigger." This disastrous strategy for handling crises, which awards the financial institutions for their incompetence and even crimes, is nothing less than economic and political suicide. "When regulations fail, or are abandoned," writes Galbraith, "bad practices spread for a simple reason: they are profitable. Market mechanisms favour them in the short run. But ultimately, if regulation fails, trust fails, and the market itself will then collapse."[18]

Let's consider briefly what the purpose for government has become at a time when the market rules everything. Today, our economic and political leaders myopically believe that government exists for four basic reasons: 1. Through the use of corporate lobbyists, eliminate all regulatory legislation on the part of the government that work to curb profits and corporate expansion both at home and abroad; 2. Provide emergency funds to banks and corporations if and when the next speculative bubble, which they deliberately create in order to stimulate massive profits, bursts; 3. Impose harsh "austerity measures" on the people by eliminating social safety nets, a strategy that supposedly attracts investment, not to mention public protests; 4. Turn the United States into a global military policeman, which, by way of robust spending on weapons and security in the perpetual "War on Terror," has spawned the biggest corporate welfare program ever conceived. It is no mistake that the average citizen is altogether absent from these four categories. As far as the corporations are concerned—and they are very concerned—the people should have no say as to how their societies are governed.

This narrow understanding of government's ultimate purpose is no longer limited to the "political thinkers" in the United States and the United Kingdom, where "free market" economics first got traction. Today, the majority of nations, in order to qualify for an emergency loan, attract foreign investment, or simply remain competitive on the international stage, are compelled to adopt the extreme liberal policies of Anglo-Saxon capitalism, where the "invisible hand of the market" is not so invisible after all. Like the

---

18   Galbraith, *The Predator State*, xv.

ancient Greek's omniscient Oracle at Delphi, the free market is believed to possess supernatural powers that no mortal being should disturb.

FREE MARKETS—FOR CORPORATIONS

For a brief moment following the global financial collapse of 2008, it looked as if the world had received a huge wakeup call and corporate power would be tamed. French President Nicolas Sarkozy, for example, believing that the people-oriented economic system had been redeemed in the wake of the global crisis, harshly criticized our take-no-prisoner free market system. During his key-note speech at the 40th World Economic Forum, he pounded the podium and defiantly declared: "From the moment we accepted the idea that the market was always right and that no other opposing factors need to be taken into account, globalization skidded out of control."[19]

Indeed, the humble pie served after the crash was large enough for everybody to have a bite. Alan Greenspan, for example, who served as the Federal Reserve chairman for eighteen years, was called to testify before the House Committee on Oversight and Government Reform on how he contributed to the epic meltdown.[20] In what should have been a wakeup call to the liberal economic reformers, Greenspan admitted he had placed too much faith in the self-correcting power of the free markets. "Yes, I've found a flaw," Greenspan conceded matter-of-factly, as if he had just discovered a fly in his soup. "I don't know how significant or permanent it is. But I've been very distressed by that fact." When pressed on the issue by the Democratic committee chairman, Henry Waxman, Greenspan admitted to a more serious flaw in his personal philosophy that unregulated free markets are a prerequisite for strong economic performance. "I made a mistake in presuming that the self-interests

---

19   Paul Armstrong, "Sarkozy Calls for Reform amid 'Crisis of Globalization,'" CNN, January 27, 2010.

20   "Waxman to Greenspan: Were You Wrong?" C-Span, YouTube: www.youtube.com/watch?v=txw4GvEFGWs, October 23, 2008.

of organizations—specifically banks and others—were such that they were best capable of protecting their own shareholders and their equity in the firms."

"In other words, you found that your view of the world, your ideology, was not right, it was not working," Waxman implored. "Absolutely, precisely," Greenspan, who could afford to be candid since he was no longer in charge of the printing presses, admitted. "You know, that's precisely the reason I was shocked, because I have been going for forty years or more with very considerable evidence that it [the financial system] was working exceptionally well."

Not everybody, however, was convinced that the free-market ride was approaching the end of the road. In fact, as the world blinked in the face of economic catastrophe, corporate power actually took a giant step forward. The journalist and author Naomi Klein was one of those who predicted at the start of the crisis that laissez-faire economics was too resilient to let one major crisis bring it down.[21] "During boom times, it's profitable to preach laissez-faire, because an absentee government allows speculative bubbles to inflate," Klein wrote. "When those bubbles burst, the ideology becomes a hindrance…while big government rides to the rescue." And that is exactly what has transpired in dramatic fashion. But does this spell the end of the laissez-faire ideology? Will our political leaders finally lead the way to a more humane economic system where the person, as opposed to the organization, is the center of the economic universe? Have we learned any lessons from the latest collapse? Better not hold your breath, Klein rightly advised.

"The ideology will come roaring back when the bailouts are done," Klein predicted. "The massive debts the public is accumulating to bail out the speculators will then become part of a global budget crisis that will be the rationalization for deep cuts to social programs, and for a renewed push to privatize what is left of the public sector." In other words, the average American is being turned into a scapegoat for the crimes committed by corporate

---

21   Naomi Klein, "Free Market Ideology Is Far from Finished," *Guardian*, September 20, 2008.

America, which is determined not to surrender any of the vast privileges it has accumulated over the years.

It is not just the financial system, however, that is failing; the judicial system is also falling far short of its duties. After all, not a single individual who knowingly dragged the economy to the brink of the abyss was punished. Well, that's not entirely true. Does anybody remember the harsh sentence handed down to Bernie Madoff, the financier who bilked thousands of clients out of billions of dollars in an elaborate Ponzi scheme? Madoff was sentenced in March 2009 to 150 years in prison! Why? Because Madoff's clients were all very wealthy; his mistake was he bilked the wrong people. On the other hand, the reason nobody did jail time for their role in wrecking the global economy, not to mention millions of American lives, was because the victims of *that* crisis were the vulnerable middle class – not the politically protected corporate class. Our government representatives simply have no incentive to protect those who are most susceptible to extreme economic fluctuations: the US middle-class taxpayer.

This pathetic state of affairs, in which investors scream about "government interference" yet demand government handouts every time they wrap the economy around a telephone pole, is an example of a free market economy at its very ugliest. It has nothing at all in common with true capitalism. Yet we simply encourage such behavior by printing more Monopoly money every time the speculators hedge their bets wrong. This is like taking a trip to Vegas knowing that the winnings are yours to keep, while all of the losses will be compensated. With a guarantee like that, who would not bet the house at the poker table? Despite this self-destructive behavior, there is no indication whatsoever that America is ready to check itself into a self-help program to treat its gambling addiction.

Meanwhile, America's loose interpretation of "free markets," which reduces society and the marketplace to the lowest common denominator, forces the entire planet to follow our lead. Despite a global economic crisis that should have tempered our faith in Anglo-Saxon capitalism, the only recourse for global leaders is to keep economic pace and political peace with the world's economic superpower. As admitted by US political guru Zbigniew Brzezinski, European governments introduce pro-business legislation because "the more competitive and even ruthless American economic culture has to be emulated if Europe is not to fall behind further."[22] European governments are now mirroring the United States by imposing harsh austerity measures on their people at the same time that unelected technocrats—much like Ben Bernanke, the Federal Reserve chairman—wield unprecedented economic and political powers in direct violation of the US Constitution. It should be noted that French President Sarkozy, who is now out of a job, beat a hasty retreat from his post crisis preaching, even ramming through harsh labor reform legislation, which included increasing the retirement age in France.

"Only a year ago Europe's leaders were laying into American free-marketry and declaring unbridled capitalism finished," the *Economist* noted with a hint of satisfaction. "The euro-zone crisis has exposed such hypocrisy."[23]

AMERICA'S "CINDERELLA STORY"

The massive denial of justice and common sense following the latest global crisis is prompting many Americans to start asking some hard questions about their socioeconomic system. For example, what is it about the US economy that has allowed it to stay ahead of the global pack for such a long time? What management practices are allowing American corporations to be the international pace car on the road to riches that other nations are reluctantly compelled to imitate? What is it about American-style capitalism that made Europeans cringe in horror in the first place? The answers to such questions may help explain the current levels of breathtaking inequality now rampant in the United States. Unknown to most Americans, there lurks a darker, more sinister side to our economic "Cinderella story"

---

22   Zbigniew Brzezinski, *The Grand Chessboard*, (New York: HarperCollins Publishers, 1997), 26.

23   Charlemagne, "Calling Time on Progress," *Economist*, July 15, 2010.

that demands deeper consideration. Although the United States is the most economically developed nation in the world, it actually has more in common with the social stratum of Mexico, for example, than that of Canada and Europe.[24] It is critical that we come to terms with this unpleasant fact if we hope to change corporate behavior. Turning over the rock of our economic system will help us to restore a sense of equality into American life once again.

First, it is important to understand that the term "economic growth," which the economists kick around with reckless abandon, is highly ambiguous and usually applies only to corporate performance, *not* the general wealth and well-being of the individual and his family. When economists want to demonstrate how well the economy is performing, they casually point to the stock market, or corporate earnings, as opposed to the wages and living standards of the middle class. In similar fashion, the pharaohs of ancient Egypt, for example, were able to point to the Great Pyramid of Cheops as an indicator of the power and wealth of their civilization. Yet this magnificent achievement, much like the stock market, tells the observer very little about the lives of the forgotten people who sacrificed their blood, sweat, and tears to construct this immense wonder.[25] It only tells the observer about the greatness of ancient Egypt per se. And so it is with modern America.

Consider the fantastic growth of billionaires in the United States over a very short time. When Forbes magazine launched its ranking of the nation's ultra wealthy in 1982, the "price of admission" into this prestigious club was just $75 million of net worth. Today, as Forbes reported, even after adjusting for inflation, "this year's entry fee ($1.1 billion) is roughly six times what it was 30 years ago."[26]

---

24 According to the US Census bureau, between 1970 and 2008 the Gini coefficient, a measure of income inequality, jumped from thirty-nine to forty-seven, which means that US inequality rates are more in line with that of Mexico, whereas Gini rates from European nations and Canada have indices between twenty-four and thirty-six, and thus far lesser rates of inequality.

25 The first workforce strike was said to have taken place under Pharaoh Ramses III in ancient Egypt in the twelfth century during construction of the royal necropolis.

26 Luisa Kroll, "The Forbes 400: The Richest People in America," *Forbes*, September 19, 2012.

Here is a look at the residents of the Forbes 400 penthouse, otherwise known as the 1 percent: "The combined net worth of the 2012 class of the 400 richest Americans is $1.7 trillion, up from $1.5 trillion a year ago. The average net worth of a Forbes 400 member is a staggering $4.2 billion, up from $3.8 billion, and the highest ever, as two-thirds of the individuals added to their fortunes in the past year."

Now compare those figures to 1982, when there were just 13 billionaires while the total worth of the 400 club was just $93 billion. Despite what the super rich wish to believe, this massive hoarding of wealth is working against the American people.

For many years US corporations have been employing a number of controversial practices that serve to inflate their profit margins, thus allowing them to maintain an edge over the rest of the world. Yet it is never acknowledged that many of these business strategies are implemented at the expense of those at the bottom of the corporate pyramid. One of those more egregious practices involves the manipulation of technological innovations for intensely private gain.

TIGHTENING THE SCREWS ON SKELETON CREWS

Today, corporate America is hauling the technological cornucopia to market, raising massive profit, while tightening the screws on workers. Many people are wondering how this is possible. The formula is simple and practically sinister: Despite an economic crisis of epic proportions, corporations continue to report high productivity rates at the very same time they are maintaining skeleton work crews. In other words, the individuals who still have jobs are picking up a lot of slack in the production chain as corporations squeeze what they can from a reduced labor force.

The *Financial Times*, in an effort to explain why US productivity rates continue to increase as unemployment rates go through the roof, pointed to a loose "hiring and firing culture" as the culprit behind the scenes. "The US, with its hiring and firing culture, has suffered sharp rises in unemployment but also achieved gains in relative and absolute productivity."[27] US productivity rates do not square with the US employment picture. "Like Europe in the 1980s, the US unemployed are finding themselves out of work for increasingly long periods. Four in 10 have been unemployed for more than six months and many more have quit the labour market entirely, with the participation rate at its lowest level since 1985," the article revealed. As of November 2012, and despite a roaring stock market, 8 % of the available workforce remains unemployed.

Alan Greenspan gave a candid explanation as to why corporate America maintains its edge over the rest of the world: "The US has benefited much more than Europe and Japan from the information technology revolution because American businesses enjoy *greater freedom to hire and fire employees.*" Greenspan conceded that the United States was the only major country to have experienced a sharp acceleration in productivity growth as a result of investment in new technology in recent years. Since these same technologies were also available to European and Japanese companies, a "significant part" of the explanation for the difference in results is because "US companies find it much easier to introduce new equipment and *displace existing workers.*"[28]

Meanwhile, the *Economist* was ringing alarm bells back in pre-crisis 2006, but of course few people paid attention. "Thanks to a jump in productivity growth after 1995, America's economy has outpaced other rich countries for a decade. Its workers now produce over 30% more each hour they work than ten years ago.... Put another way, the typical worker earns only 10% more in real terms than his counterpart 25 years ago, even though overall productivity has risen much faster."[29] That deserves repeating: Fewer Americans are producing more goods than their predecessors,

---

27   Chris Giles, Krishna Guha, and Ralph Atkins, "At the Sharp End," *Financial Times,* January 22, 2010.

28   "Flexibility of Labour Key to US Success," *Financial Times,* July 12, 2000, 12. italics added.

29   "The Rich, the Poor and the Growing Gap between Them," *The Economist,* "Special Report: Inequality in America," June 17, 2006, 24, 25.

and getting paid less for their contributions. This largely explains why "America's economy has outpaced other rich countries for a decade." The trend continues today, yet rarely do the American media report on what can only be described as an attack on basic human rights. Three years after the above report was released, corporations continue to slash labor costs at the very same time that productivity rates are going through the roof. Needless to say, a disproportionate amount of the profits generated by these cut-throat methods are being pocketed by the golden 1 percent.

In order to appreciate how and why American workers are suffering in 2012, it is necessary to rewind the clock a bit; after all, economics is largely based on examining trends. "Businesses are squeezing more out of their downsized workforces," *USA Today* reported, quoting from the Bureau of Labor Statistics. "Labor productivity climbed at an impressive 6.2% annual rate, and labor costs fell 4.4% during fourth-quarter 2009. In the last four quarters, productivity has grown 5.1%, the fastest pace in nearly eight years."[30] The article then attempts to explain the "contradiction" of high productivity rates existing side by side high unemployment levels and a red-hot stock market. After all, it would seem logical that companies would hire more employees if production rates and consumer demand justify a larger workforce. Unfortunately, however, logic has no place in our brave new economy. Common sense and prudence has been jettisoned as companies now opt to get more productivity—and, of course, profits—from fewer and fewer workers. That dangerous trend continues unchallenged today.

"As the economy emerges from the worst recession since the 1930s, companies have been reluctant to hire workers, choosing instead to get more output from their existing staff," the *USA Today* article continues. Then, in an effort to find a silver lining in the clouds, the report actually applauds a "1% increase in the number of hours employees worked, the first gain since the second quarter of 2007." Although few workers would celebrate an

---

30 Paul Wiseman, "Productivity Rises at 6.2% Annual Rate; Jobless Claims Up," *USA Today*, February 4, 2010.

increase in their working hours, the theory is that if the amount of time employees spend on the job is increasing, this means that management will come to the conclusion that more employees are needed and a new wave of corporate hiring will commence. In reality, however, the very opposite thing is happening. Companies are increasingly reluctant to hire more employees at a time when productivity is on the rise, the number of full-time salaried employees is down, and unions are mere shadows of their former selves. And who can really blame them? After all, why spend the extra cash on hiring more workers when companies can get away with skeleton crews to haul in the harvest?

Eventually, of course, some companies will be forced to hire, but they are under no compelling obligation to do so. In fact, such a perfect storm of "positive" data (high productivity, low labor costs, silenced unions) practically guarantees that corporations will do the very opposite of what is ethically and economically expected (i.e., hire more workers), and that is to continue squeezing as much juice from their already shriveled workforce for as long as humanly possible. And that is exactly the conclusion the *USA Today* article is forced to make. Instead of corporations rushing to sort through their piled-up résumés to fill the worker-productivity deficit left by the eight million jobs lost between December 2007 and August 2009, it is reported instead that: "The number of people filing unemployment claims for the first time rose by 8,000 to 480,000 the week ending Jan. 30 [2010]; economists had expected the figure to drop last week."

A report by CNN summed up the reason for high unemployment figures in one succinct sentence: "The problem with bringing down the stubbornly high unemployment rate is that employers are learning to do more with less." [31] Isn't that nice? It is probably safe to assume that most people are also "learning to do more with less." For the average working family, however, doing "more with less" invariably means cutting back on the essentials. For corporate America, "tightening the belt" has an uncanny way of translating into higher profits and stock market earnings, especially when

---

31   Chris Isodore, "Why Employers Won't Hire," CNNMoney, December 3, 2010.

a major layoff is announced. The CNN article goes on to cite a report by the US Labor Department that showed a loss of 28,000 retail jobs for November 2010, that month's weakest showing in retail payrolls in twenty-nine years. Meanwhile, the latest reading on productivity, which tracks the economic output of each hour Americans work during a quarter, was up 2.5% in the third quarter of 2010 compared with the previous year, the Labor Department reported. This was the sixth straight quarter of productivity gains of that level or more.

So how is corporate America faring through all of this? As to be expected, like a ship on the high seas with the wind at its back. In August 2011, with the unemployment rate stuck at 9.2 percent, many US corporations were reporting stellar results. "Of the companies in the Standard & Poor 500 list of large-cap firms which have reported their quarterly earnings to date, 72 percent have beaten analysts' forecasts," Agence France-Presse reported, quoting Howard Silverblatt, an S&P analyst. "Earnings are basically the only thing holding up the market at this point," Silverblatt said. "They're amazing numbers."[32]

Despite the "amazing numbers," it now takes almost forty weeks for the unemployed to find new work, which invariably translates into less pay and benefits when and if they land a new job. Meanwhile, many individuals—who no longer appear in the official employment data—have dropped out of the labor market altogether. This represents the rise of a whole new segment of long-term unemployed Americans who are forced to become dependent on friends and family for support. More Americans have moved back in with their parents than ever before. The reason for this crippling stagnation of the labor markets is simply corporate greed, which is only concerned with serving itself.

"Just consider the main measure of corporate health: profits," writes David Leonhardt in the *New York Times*. "In Canada, Japan and most of Europe, corporate profits have still not recovered to pre-crisis levels. In the United States, profits have more than recov-

---

32   "US Company Profits Surge, Even as Economy Slows," Agence France-Presse, August 2, 2011.

ered, rising 12 percent since late 2007." Despite the fact that the global economic crisis had its roots in the United States, the real culprits behind this epic event barely flinched. As Leonhardt concludes: "For corporate America, the Great Recession is over. For the American work force, it's not."[33]

Historically, workplace innovations have been the leading factor for increasing productivity, increasing profits and, occasionally, increasing unemployment levels. And due to our love affair with everything mechanical, workers have come to understand the futility of railing against technological revolutions like modern-day Luddites. Indeed, we accept new workplace innovations as naturally as if they were another part of nature's evolutionary process. "The law of [technological] acceleration," Henry Adams boldly declared, "definite and constant as any law of mechanics, cannot be supposed to relax its energy to suit the convenience of man."[34]

But if technological development is never supposed to relax in order to "suit the convenience of man," then what is the purpose of creating a machine-dominated world in the first place? After all, humans are not machines, yet we are expected to keep constant pace with mechanical revolutions like mindless robots. "Modern science," Hannah Arendt wrote, "...has changed and reconstructed the world we live in so radically that it could be argued that the layman and the humanist, still trusting their common sense and communicating in everyday language, are out of touch with reality."[35] Today, corporate leaders have lost touch with reality and punish their workers every time a new technological innovation is introduced into the workplace. Technology is not the culprit, but rather the individuals who manipulate it for private gain at the expense of society. Corporations get away with this egregious behavior simply because we lack the institutional mechanism—that is, democracy—for keeping them under control.

33   David Leonhardt, "In Wreckage of Lost Jobs, Lost Power," *New York Times*, January 19, 2011.

34   Henry Adams, *The Education of Henry Adams* (Boston: 1918), Chapter 3, xxxiv.

35   Hannah Arendt, *Between Past and Future* (London: Faber and Faber, 1954), 268.

THE END OF BUSINESS AS USUAL

At this point, it may be reasonable to ask whether the "global financial crisis" itself is to blame for our present economic doldrums, or if there is something much deeper at work. Indeed, there seems to have been a tectonic shift in the way corporate America now prefers to do business. Robert Reich, former US secretary of labor, warned before the latest economic storm made landfall that middle-class families "have exhausted the coping mechanisms they have used for more than three decades to get by on median wages that are barely higher than they were in 1970, adjusted for inflation…[Y]et for years now, America's middle class has lived beyond its pay cheque. Middle-class lifestyles have flourished even though median wages have barely budged. That is ending and Americans are beginning to feel the consequences."[36] Given such dire conditions, Washington is trying to coax corporate America to open the purse strings and expand its payrolls.

In December 2010, the White House, fully aware that long-term high unemployment is nothing less than political suicide, invited twenty corporate leaders to a meeting with President Barack Obama. The purpose of the "working lunch" was to hash out ways to get the economy rolling again; Obama appealed to the company heads to consider hiring again. After all, the Democratic leader had agreed to the multibillion-dollar bailout that kept the ship of corporate America afloat. Certainly he is entitled to make some requests, right? The assembled CEOs, however, proved the adage that nothing is rarer in politics than gratitude. Indeed, the corporate chiefs wasted the afternoon complaining about "low consumer demand" and "stifling government regulations" as to why they are averse to hiring more employees.[37] This is simply putting the cart before the horse. After all, consumer spending will remain in the basement so long as the people who make up the consumers, namely the workers, continue to be underpaid and

---

36   Robert Reich, "America's Middle Classes Are No Longer Coping," *Financial Times*, January, 29, 2007, 11.
37   Richard Wolf, David Jackson, Matt Kranz, and Laura Petrecca, "Obama Meets with CEOs to Urge Them to Start Hiring," *USA Today*, December 12, 2010.

jobless. To put it another way, the multibillion-dollar "stimulus package" awarded to the business community has done nothing to stimulate consumers simply because the mother lode of those emergency funds remains stuck in the pipes of the corporate penthouse. There has been no trickle-down effect, not even a sign of water damage in the ceiling above our heads.

(Incidentally, with transnational corporations acting as political animals in their own right, it does not seem too outrageous to suggest that some right-leaning CEOs—and it seems the majority of them do lean in that direction—choose to suppress hiring in order to manipulate the political winds. After all, why hire additional workers if that would only benefit a politician whose policies do not reflect those of a particular corporate leader? Why hire additional employees in an election year if that would harm the "favored" candidate's chances of being elected?)

Business leaders fail to connect the dots between how employees are treated and how consumers spend their money; corporations seem to have forgotten that workers and consumers are one in the same thing (it is also worth mentioning that the transnational corporations are also consumers in their own right, and their weighty participation in the marketplace helps to drive up consumer prices). Employees, despite their valuable contributions to the success of the corporation, are treated like expendable commodities, practical liabilities, which, once made redundant, will boost stock prices.

Meanwhile, as business leaders continue to suppress hiring, more than just corporate earnings are going through the roof. In fact, the very sectors of the economy that were blamed for leading the global economy down a blind alley still got a Christmas gift, and we are not talking about a tie or sweater. Despite being in the middle of America's worst economic downturn since the Depression, "three dozen of the top publicly held securities and investment-services firms...are set to pay $144 billion in compensation and benefits this year, a 4% increase from the $139 billion paid out in 2009."[38]

---

38   Liz Rappaport, Aaron Lucchetti, and Stephen Grocer, "Wall Street Pay: A Record $144 Billion," *Wall Street Journal*, October 11, 2010.

In addition to handing out cash-filled Christmas stockings to cronies, corporate America has found other creative ways of spending its taxpayer-sponsored slush funds. Although they are sitting on veritable mountains of hard cash,[39] top executives are behaving no better than cannibals, ploughing their hoarded dollars right back into the purchase of their own company stock in the hope of artificially stimulating share prices. Now, what would make them do such a thing? "Sitting on these unprecedented levels of cash, U.S. companies are buying back their own stock in droves," reported the *Washington Post*. "So far this year, firms have announced they will purchase $273 billion of their own shares, more than five times as much compared with this time last year."[40] Yes, you have read correctly: At a time of high unemployment and high productivity rates, American CEOs have purchased more than a quarter of a trillion dollars of their own company stocks.

While obsessed with helping themselves and their top shareholders, corporate leaders are neglecting to spend their cash on the "job-generating activities that could produce economic growth," the article noted. As the American people are stuck holding the bill for bailing out the captains of industry—"socialism for the rich, capitalism for the poor," as the saying goes—we are rewarded for our long-term tax debt by "austerity measures," which include high unemployment, stunted wages, dismal benefit programs, and paltry investment into job training.

Even the *Wall Street Journal* admitted that this "recovery" has shown precious little benefits for the average person. "From mid-2009 through the end of 2010, output per hour at U.S. nonfarm businesses rose 5.2% as companies found ways to squeeze more from their existing workers," wrote Mark Whitehouse in his *WSJ* analytical blog. "But the lion's share of that gain went to share-

---

39   According to Moody's Investors Service, the total cash held by US nonfinancial corporations surged to $1.2 trillion at the end of 2010, an increase of 11.2 percent from a year earlier. Reported in AFP article (above) "US Company Profits Surge, Even as Economy Slows."

40   Jia Lynn Yang, "U.S. Companies Buy Back Stock in Droves as They Hold Record Levels of Cash," *Washington Post*, October 7, 2010.

holders in the form of record profits, rather than to workers in the form of raises. Hourly wages, adjusted for inflation, rose only 0.3%, according to the Labor Department."[41] The conclusion from the data shows how insanely greedy corporations have become since the end of World War II, and especially since the Reagan era. "In other words," Whitehouse concludes, "companies shared only 6% of productivity gains with their workers [compared with] 58% since records began in 1947." Yet corporate executives have the nerve to complain that consumers are not spending their money.

Meanwhile, with a soaring stock market and extreme executive pay the only real signs of a recovery, an increasing number of Americans are failing to keep the roof over their heads. A study put out by the American Association of Retired Persons (AARP) painted a dire picture of US home ownership, even among the senior citizens: "As of December 2011, approximately 3.5 million loans of people age 50+ were underwater—meaning homeowners owe more than their home is worth, so they have no equity; 600,000 loans of people age 50+ were in foreclosure, and another 625,000 loans were 90 or more days delinquent. From 2007 to 2011, more than 1.5 million older Americans lost their homes as a result of the mortgage crisis."[42] Meanwhile, the Commerce Department, in its report on new home sales for July 2010, showed the worst figures since 1963, the same year that President John F. Kennedy famously remarked that a "rising tide lifts all boats." Who can even afford to buy a boat these days? Americans losing their homes is a truly disturbing scenario for no other purchase symbolizes individual freedom and success better than home ownership.

Clearly, the reason why so many Americans are failing to maintain living standards comparable with that of past generations is that corporations refuse to share the cornucopia of wealth that the seeds of technology have produced. This should not be confused as some sort of call for "redistributing the wealth," but rather reinvesting in the American Dream. After all, for many

---

41   Mark Whitehouse, "Number of the Week: Workers Not Benefitting from Productivity Gains," *Wall Street Journal*/blog, March 5, 2011.
42   Lori A. Trawinski, Ph.D, "Nightmare on Main Street: Older Americans and the Mortgage Crisis," AARP Public Policy Institute, July 2012.

seasons American workers have tilled and turned the fields of their corporate overlords. But now that it is time to bring in the lucrative harvest, American workers are told they are longer needed. Thanks to the explosion of a real estate bubble courtesy of the banking community, it is the "small people" who must suffer the full brunt of layoffs, reduced wages, and major cutbacks on social services and other benefits at a time when they are needed the most. This type of reckless behavior is not capitalism; it is simply highway robbery carried out by individuals whose insatiable greed prevents them from doing the right thing.

For too long corporate America has been putting the squeeze on two categories of Americans: those with jobs and those without jobs. While a large percentage of the workforce is now unemployed, those with jobs are working longer hours and producing more goods. No wonder so many Americans can't get a break today.

WHERE'S THE BEACH?

In light of all the extra work that US workers are now performing, it might be expected that they are receiving attractive vacation packages. In fact, nothing could be further from the truth. US corporations have turned employee vacations into some sort of a privilege as opposed to the necessity they are. "The United States is practically the only developed country in the world that doesn't require companies to give their workers time off," revealed an article in *The Atlantic*. "In Germany, workers are guaranteed a month. In the UK, they're guaranteed more than five weeks of paid vacation. In the US...there is no such guarantee." [43]

According to an exhaustive report by the Center for American Progress,[44] US citizens "work longer hours than workers in most other developed countries, including Japan, where there is even a

---

43   Derek Thompson, "The Only Advanced Country without a National Vacation Policy? It's the U.S.," *The Atlantic*, November 23, 2012.

44   Joan C. Williams and Heather Boushey, "The Three Faces of Work-Family Conflict," Center for American Progress, January 2010.

word, *karoshi,* for 'death by overwork.' The typical American middle-income family put in an average of 11 more hours a week in 2006 than it did in 1979."[45] Not only are American families working longer hours, thereby contributing to higher levels of "work-family conflicts," they do so without government-mandated support of working families. The Center for American Progress report highlights the following grim facts about the pressure-cooker atmosphere now prevailing inside the US economy: "Only the United States lacks paid maternity-leave laws among the 30 industrialized democracies in the Organization for Economic Cooperation and Development.[46] The only family leave available is unpaid, limited to three months, and covers only about half of the labor force. Discrimination against workers with family responsibilities, illegal throughout Europe,[17] is forbidden only indirectly here. Americans also lack paid sick days, limits on mandatory overtime, the right to request work-time flexibility without retaliation, and proportional wages for part-time work."

Meanwhile, efforts on the part of a few brave politicians rarely get noticed. For example, legislation introduced by former Congressman Alan Grayson (D-Florida), entitled "Paid Vacation Act of 2009," which would have required corporations to provide at least one week of paid annual leave, fizzled out on the floor thanks to fearmongering from the pro-business congressional chorus who practically connected vacation time with communism. According to a CNN report, "Opponents said that [the legislation] would have a negative impact on business and that the government shouldn't

---

45   Organization for Economic Cooperation and Development (OECD), OECD Stat Extracts, Average annual hours actually worked per individual worker, http://stats.oecd.org/Index.aspx?DatasetCode=ANHRS (data shows United States among top eleven countries with longest work hours, and longer work hours than Japan from period between 2000 to 2008).

46   Rebecca Ray, Janet C. Gornick, and John Schmitt, Center for Economic and Policy Research, "Parental Leave Policies in 21 Countries: Assessing Generosity and Gender Equality" (2008, Rev. June 2009), available at www.lisproject.org/publications/parental-work/ParentLeave Report.pdf

47   Ariane Hegewich and Janet C. Gornick, Institute for Women's Policy Research & Center for WorkLife Law, "Statutory Routes to Workplace Flexibility in Cross-National Perspective 15" (2008), available at http://worklifelaw.org/pubs/Statutory%20Routes%20to%20WkFlex.pdf.

get involved in the workplace."[48] Except when it comes to bailing them out of bankruptcy, that is.

In American society, the denial of basic human rights is explained away as due to some sort of predilection for supreme sacrifice on the part of the American people. US workers, as the fairy tale goes, are hardwired for hard work, which makes us somehow more predisposed to prefer the office over a beach getaway with the family. In fact, Americans are made to feel guilty for taking what is rightfully theirs: a break from the monotony of labor in order to enjoy time with the family. According to a report in the *American Prospect*, "A third fewer American families take vacations together today than they did in 1970." [49] The abovementioned article in *The Atlantic*, meanwhile, revealed that "57% of Americans had up to two weeks of unused vacation time at the end of 2011," and that "Americans work longer hours than practically any advanced country except South Korea and Japan."

Despite all the hype about the American people's "Protestant work ethic" and industriousness, Americans are not much different from people elsewhere in the world when it comes to wanting a break from work. We are not robots, nor are we masochists. In fact, the blustery rhetoric about "Americans' devotion to work" has more to do with the lack of political will and excessive corporate influence than any intimate attachment to our desks. The last piece of government legislation to help Americans maintain a healthy and sane balance between work and family life was the Family and Medical Leave Act, passed in 1993. Since then, the world seems to have passed us by. Once again, America's supine labor movement plays a large role in keeping vacation time in the United States to exactly zero. "The weak labor movement in the U.S. is partly to blame for the stingy federal policies around vacation and holidays," as reported in the Society Pages. "The U.S. federal government dictates that employees are given exactly zero paid holiday and vacation days a year (that means, if you get such

---

48   A. Pawlowski, "Why Is America the 'No-Vacation Nation'?" CNN, May 23, 2011.

49   Courtney E. Martin, "Time Off for the Overworked American," *American Prospect*, May 21, 2007.

things, it is because your employer is being generous)."[50] The article reveals what many Americans simply do not know: Among all OECD countries, every country except Canada and Japan (and the United States) receives at least twenty mandatory paid vacation days per year. Americans are guaranteed nothing. This also includes, incidentally, any sort of paid parental leave.

The irony is that much of the extra cash that companies think they are saving by playing Ebenezer Scrooge goes up in smoke due to the negative side effects of an overworked, overstressed workforce. Statistics regularly show that job-related stress expenditures cost businesses hundreds of billions of dollars every year in absenteeism, lost productivity, and health costs. At the same time, the overwhelming majority of visits to primary care physicians are related to stress-induced issues. Nearly one in five Americans (40 million people) suffer from anxiety disorders, "the most common class of psychiatric ailment we have."[51] And there is no need to mention the tragic incidences of individuals "going postal" at the office over the most trivial issues. It would not seem unreasonable to trace at least part of the source of this destructive behavior back to stressful workplace conditions.

Now let's briefly imagine what would happen if businesses were suddenly required by law to grant their employees additional vacation time. This would force corporations to do exactly what they should have been doing all along: hire more workers. Corporate America would be forced to bring on board additional employees to fill in for those individuals who would be legally required to bask in the sun in some tropical clime (and spend money, by the way, which could also provide a boost to the economy. After all, workers are also consumers—but only when they have the time and money that permits them to consume. There could even be tax breaks for families that take their vacation inside the United States.). This is one obvious way to offset America's unprecedentedly high unemployment figures.

---

50   Lisa Wade, "Paid Holidays/Vacation Days in the U.S. Versus Other OECD Countries," www.thesocietypages.org, January 31, 2010.
51   Maura Kelly, "Trickle-Down Distress: How America's Broken Meritocracy Drives Our National Anxiety Epidemic," *The Atlantic*, July 7, 2012.

There would also be an increase in the time children and parents spend together. Ironically, the United States is very generous when it comes to offering summer breaks to its student body, yet has no problem with American workers receiving the stingiest vacation packages in the developed world. The equation is severely backward. Think about it: Does it make sense that our children are sitting at home for three months out of the summer, oftentimes without any adult supervision, while their parents are sitting at work with no hope of a vacation?

Mandatory vacation time would allow Americans to relax. After all, it cannot be mere coincidence that the most overworked people on the planet also experience the highest incidences of workplace violence. It is high time that the biggest gun culture in the world permits its people to hit the beach once in a while. Yet employer-based studies continue to focus their myopic vision on a host of other problems that spark workplace violence, including "domestic issues," as if stress at work is some sort of abstract part of the equation, or that domestic issues never arise from dismal workplace conditions. The simple solution of providing American workers with the necessary free time away from the office or factory has failed to click. After all, it is no secret that a well-rested employee is more productive on the job and less prone to harbor ill feelings for the employing company. All things considered, employers do not save anything by depriving their workforce of leisure time. Corporations need to heed the advice of the philosopher Immanuel Kant, who advised that "man must be treated as an end and not as a means."[52]

WALL STREET'S ROCKET SCIENTISTS

One reason the financial markets tanked in 2008 is that the people selling the high-risk investment schemes don't have the slightest clue as to how their products work. That is because Wall

---

52   George Sabine and Thomas Thorson, *A History of Political Theory*, fourth edition (Harcourt Brace Publishers, 1973), 162–163.

Street has been recruiting veritable rocket scientists to devise the latest Ponzi scheme. "Ever wonder how investment bankers…ever invented products like those crazily sophisticated, synthetic collateralized debt obligations that brought down the financial system?" asked *Time* magazine. "Well, they didn't. They hired rocket scientists to do that—a whole lot of them. In fact, Wall Street hires more math, engineering and science graduates than the semiconductor industry, Big Pharma or the telecommunications business."[53]

There are two immediate problems with Wall Street absorbing so many math and engineering wizards. First, it is making the world of investment unnecessarily complicated, to the point where not even the bankers understand what they are selling to investors. And if the bankers cannot sense that the products they are hawking to unsuspecting buyers are fatally flawed then we will continue to have major disruptions of our economic system. The next time around, however, there may not be enough dollars in the cash register to plug the hole.

More important, however, Wall Street is creating a huge brain drain on the research and development sectors that are responsible for stimulating new industries and, by way of extension, job growth. Instead of our "rocket scientists" working to create the next-generation electric automobile, solar fuel cells or wind farms, for example, technologies that have the capacity to radically transform our society and economy (not to mention our presently unsustainable lifestyles), they are working on ways to lure investors into risky investment plans. The above article from *Time*, citing a study from the Kauffman Foundation, reports that "the financial sector is sucking talent and entrepreneurial energy from the more socially beneficial sectors of the economy." It cites statistics from two of America's leading universities, Harvard, where the graduates "enter financial occupations at a far higher rate now than they did in the 1970s," and MIT, where the proportion of graduates who opted for Wall Street "rose from 18% in 2003 to 25% in 2006." You do not have to be a mathematician to appreciate the significance of these numbers.

---

53   Rana Foroohar, "The Great Wall Street Sucking Sound," *Time*, March 2011.

This internal brain drain is robbing the US economy of the new industries that have been the engine of growth in the past. Wall Street is getting trapped in a vicious cycle where it is cannibalizing the most crucial part of the US economy—the talented individuals who introduce the transformative, job-creating industries that we need. Meanwhile, as there will naturally become a shortage of ways to separate investors from their money, Wall Street will have no other choice but to compromise itself in extremely risky business transactions, like promoting worthless mortgages to investors.

TAKE THE MONEY AND RUN

At the very same time that corporate America is depriving employees of the right to some rest and relaxation it is deporting many of our best jobs overseas. Thousands of companies once rooted firmly in the United States are taking advantage of open-door policies (which have a tendency for opening in just one direction) that fail to punish corporations that run away to greener fields for their labor requirements. According to one government estimate, more than 2,500 US corporations have a total of 23,853 overseas affiliations, providing jobs for 9.5 million workers and sales to the tune of $4.1 trillion.[54] "These companies have used the sharp downturn as an opportunity to cull their payrolls for good," argues Robert Reich, "substituting labor-saving technologies and outsourcing to workers abroad or to contract workers here."[55]

Meanwhile, it is not difficult to guess where many American products—now being produced dirt cheap by US labor—are going. Yes, overseas, where foreign customers blessed with American jobs can afford to spend. "The big growth is happening outside the US, not in the US, and you've seen a lot of companies increase their export sales as a percentage of the total," Marc

---

54   Bureau of Economic Analysis, US Commerce Department, Survey of Current Business, November 2008, Table 17.2, 43.
55   Robert Reich, "Entrepreneur or Unemployed," *New York Times,* June 1, 2010.

Pado, US market strategist for Cantor Fitzgerald, told Agence France-Presse.[56]

This writer experienced the corporate cut-and-run campaign firsthand in the early 1990s when AT&T was just beginning to introduce its revolutionary "voice-recognition" technologies and telephone operators were being tossed aside like yesterday's obsolete gadget. After spending years on the job, answering up to 1,200 calls per day, tens of thousands of operators were made redundant once the automated call systems were able to mimic the human role of providing "quality service." Any person who has experienced the frustration of being put on hold or "assisted" by touch-tone commands that all too often end up in an electronic cul-de-sac somewhere overseas understands at least half of the story. This loss of thousands of call center jobs in the United States to foreign shores, however, has practically lost relevancy since "call centre workers are becoming as cheap to hire in the US as they are in India," as the *Financial Times* reported.[57]

Brace yourself because the madness is just beginning. Does anybody recall how much Bank of America received after the crash and burn of the US financial sector? BOA got a whopping $45 billion courtesy of Joe Taxpayer. So how did BOA return the favor? America's second-largest bank is relocating its business-support operations to the Philippines, *Mother Jones* revealed. "Bank of America, which last fall announced plans to lay off 30,000 workers, is about to go on a hiring spree—overseas," the journal reported. "Needless to say, the outsourcing is bad news for an already hurting US call center industry, which has shed some 500,000 jobs during the past four years."[58] If this is really how globalization works, shouldn't we start demanding a refund?

The damage to the heart of American productivity is certainly not limited to the service sector. Former politician and author

---

56   "US Company Profits Surge, Even as Economy Slows," Agence France-Presse, August, 2, 2011.

57   James Lamont, "US Matches Indian Call Centre Costs," *Financial Times*, August 17, 2010.

58   Josh Harkinson, "3 Years after Taxpayer Bailout, Bank of America Ships Jobs Overseas," *Mother Jones*, May 29, 2012.

Patrick J. Buchanan turned a spotlight on the "tsunami of imports" and its grievous effects on American employment prospects. "During the first decade of the twenty-first century, U.S. semiconductor and electronic components producers lost 42 percent of their jobs; communications equipment producers lost 48 percent of their jobs; textile and apparel producers lost, respectively, 63 percent and 61 percent of their jobs."[59] This loss of American factory jobs, which could signal the real collapse of US global prestige, has been happening for almost half a century. As one observer reported: "Although the number of jobs in American manufacturing was rather constant at about 17 million from 1969 to 2002, manufacturing's share of jobs continued to decline from about 28% in 1962 to only 9% in 2011."[60]

Incidentally, despite accumulating astronomical profit on its overseas ventures, corporate America is lobbying for another "tax holiday" so it can haul the booty home at a big discount. But how did big business use the last tax holiday? It most certainly did not open any new factories or invest in employee training programs. According to a report in the *New York Times*, quoting studies from the National Bureau of Economic Research, "the last tax holiday, enacted in 2004, largely failed to spur investment or job growth. Companies spent most of the repatriated $300 billion on dividends and stock buybacks, enriching executives and shareholders."[61]

Meanwhile, the outsourcing debate is not simply a question of sending good American jobs overseas while damaging the home economy. US corporations, dangling the possibility of citizenship as bait, are luring foreign workers to the United States to take advantage of cheap labor. In 2009 alone, as unemployment was hitting record levels, 1,130,000 green cards were issued, with 808,000 going to permanent immigrants of working age.[62] Yet our

---

59   Patrick J. Buchanan, *Suicide of a Superpower* (New York: St. Martin's Press, 2011), 13–14, quoting from Mark Drajem, "China's Trade Gap with U.S. Climbs to Record, Fueling Yuan Tension," Bloomberg.com, Oct.14, 2010.
60   Gary Becker, "A Farewell to Factories," MarketWatch, April 24, 2012.
61   "No Holiday," Editorial, *New York Times*, October 23, 2011.
62   Department of Homeland Security, "Persons Obtaining Legal Permanent Resident Status by Gender, Age, Marital Status and Occupation; Fiscal Year 2009," www.dhs.gov.

business leaders continue to deny that this phenomenon is in any way responsible for disrupting the economy.

The US government allows companies to invite high-skill workers to our country if they qualify for so-called H1B and L-1 guest worker visas, which permit foreigners to live and work in the United States for up to six years maximum, but under strict guidelines. First, since the employer (as opposed to the applicant or government) is in physical possession of the work permit, guest workers can change jobs only in very limited circumstances, and their employer can terminate the visa at any time; in such cases, the guest worker is required to leave the country. This relationship between employer and guest worker, which leaves all the power in the hands of the former, opens the door to all sorts of problems.

"In contrast to the employment rights of citizens and permanent residents, H-1B and L-1 rules place most of the power in the hands of the employer...and create sizeable opportunities for the exploitation of guest workers," according to a report by the Economic Policy Institute (EPI). "Many have described this employment relationship as indentured servitude."[63] The Louisiana Federation of Teachers, for example, recently filed a complaint on behalf of teachers brought to the United States from the Philippines, who were kept under conditions of "virtual servitude." It was reported that they were intimidated, charged excessive rates for their necessities, and forced to live in run-down dwellings leased by their employer.[64]

At the same time, corporations are even abusing international work-travel programs for students in an effort to inflate their bottom line. Each year thousands of students from around the world travel to the United States on J-1 visas to learn about life in America, immerse themselves in the culture, and make lasting friendships. This requires that they work for two months at a US company to defray the costs of their travels and rent. According to one recent news report, however, these students are practically

---

63   Ron Hira, "Bridge to Immigration or Cheap Temporary Labor?" *Economic Policy Institute*, February 17, 2010, 2.
64   Gregg Toppo and Icess Fernandez, "Federal Complaint: Filipino Teachers Held in 'Servitude,'" *USA Today*, October 27, 2009.

being used as slave labor, which caused one group to walk off their jobs at a Hershey plant in Palmyra, Pennsylvania.

As the *New York Times* reported: "Hundreds of foreign students, waving their fists and shouting defiantly in many languages, walked off their jobs on Wednesday at a plant here that packs Hershey's chocolates, saying a summer program that was supposed to be a cultural exchange instead turned them into underpaid labor."[65] The article went on to reveal that the once-reputable program "has drawn complaints from students about low wages and unexpectedly difficult work conditions." The Palmyra plant walkout is the first time, however, that foreign students "engaged in a strike to protest their employment."

Now, if corporate America is willing to force young students from abroad into what amounts to servitude, then imagine how it treats its own workers who have no organized voice? While such cases of abuse demand an investigation, what must concern us here is how such legislation works to the disadvantage of the domestic workforce. In the case of the H-1B and L-1 non-immigrant visas, these are significant guest worker programs, "admitting 214,261 new foreign workers in fiscal year 2008 alone, a year in which the U.S. economy lost a net of 920,000 jobs."[66] Obviously, these are much different visas from a "cultural exchange" program for students. Meanwhile, the exact number of guest workers in the United States at any given time is unknown because, according to the EPI report, "the government does not track those numbers." It has been estimated, however, that there are some 600,000 H-1B and 350,000 L-1 visa holders working in the United States at any given time.

The report notes that the majority of these guest workers never achieve the dream of acquiring US citizenship. They are herded to the United States, where they perform their duties for much less than what an American requires for his basic needs, and then sent back home. The conclusion that the EPI report arrives at is disconcerting both for the guest workers, who earn less than the

---

65 Julia Preston, "Foreign Students in Work Visa Program Stage Walkout at Plant," *New York Times*, August 17, 2011.

66 Hira, page 3.

going rate for the tasks they are performing, and for the domestic workforce, which is being overlooked and "undercut" due to this vast pool of foreign talent that corporations are now farming.

"The very large number of H-1B and L-1 workers, coupled with the smaller allotment of employment-based immigration visas, often put guest workers who want to become permanent residents in a state of indentured limbo," the report says. It then concludes with a nice suggestion: "When employers need skilled foreign workers, they should rely on permanent immigration to supply them. Guest worker visa programs should be relied on only when truly necessary and should be significantly overhauled to ensure that foreign workers cannot be exploited and American workers are not undercut."[67]

Clearly, the manipulation of foreign workers, both at home and abroad, has worked to the general disadvantage of the native workforce while the corporations reap fantastic rewards. And who could fail to enjoy the irony of capitalist nations filling their labor quotas from nations *created under the banners of socialism and communism.* Why are native-born Americans not filling the available job openings? Why did the government liberally give away 10,300,000 green cards to foreigners between 2000-2010?[68] Considering that Americans are weathering through the worst economic storm since the Great Depression, isn't it time we lend our unconditional support to US labor?

TIME TO GRAB A PITCHFORK?

Given this aggressive corporate environment, which treats labor as a means as opposed to an end, more and more people are venting their outrage on the street. Moreover, the unprecedented level of income disparity—in the middle of a deep recession, no less—is starting to reopen the archaic debate on "class" and "class warfare," which, ironically, was one of the reasons that European

---

67   Hira, page 13. In a footnote to this paragraph, Hira notes that the programs are "also being used to substitute younger workers for older incumbent ones."
68   Buchanan, *Suicide of a Superpower*, p.14.

immigrants risked a transatlantic voyage to America in the first place. Yet it is not angry mobs with pitchforks that are uttering such unsavory thoughts, but some of the wealthiest Americans. This should come as no surprise since it is the excessively wealthy who stand to lose the most in the event of a real social crisis.

George Soros, the billionaire investor who is known for singlehandedly breaking the Bank of England, told the *Daily Beast* that the current economic situation "is about as serious and difficult as I've experienced in my career." Soros goes on to warn of civil unrest and violence on US streets, a real "class war," which could severely curtail our already weakened civil liberties. "It [the civil unrest] will be an excuse for cracking down and using strong-arm tactics to maintain law and order, which…could bring about a repressive political system, a society where individual liberty is much more constrained."[69]

Warren Buffett, the billionaire chief executive of Berkshire Hathaway, also openly contemplated the specter of class warfare, albeit it with an unexpected twist. "There's class warfare, all right," Buffett admitted. "But it's my class, the rich class, that's making the war, and we're winning."[70] On another occasion, the American tycoon has said that the upper-tier segment of US society should have to bear more of the tax load, an idea that will be considered in a later chapter.

Buffett's candid assessment of income disparity in the United States was supported by a shocking article in *Foreign Affairs*: "[I]n the midst of all this misery," writes Robert C. Lieberman, professor of political science and public affairs at Columbia University, the "wealthiest Americans, among them presumably the very titans of global finance whose misadventures brought about the financial meltdown, got richer; a lot richer. In 2009, the average income of the top five percent of earners went up, while on average everyone else's income went down. This was not an anomaly but rather a continuation of a 40-year trend of ballooning incomes at the very top

---

69   John Arlidge, "George Soros on the Coming U.S. Class War," *Daily Beast*, January 23, 2012.

70   Ben Stein, "In Class Warfare, Guess Which Class Is Winning," *New York Times*, November 26, 2006.

and stagnant incomes in the middle and at the bottom. The share of total income going to the top one percent has increased from roughly eight percent in the 1960s to more than 20 percent today."[71]

Finally, there was Klaus Schwab, the founder of the World Economic Forum, where the global movers and shakers meet each year on the ski slopes of Davos, in the Swiss Alps. "Capitalism, in its current form, no longer fits the world around us," Schwab pronounced in early 2012. "We have failed to learn the lessons from the financial crisis."[72]

Despite these bracing moments of startling frankness, the negative data continue to flow as the financial burden on Main Street, America, multiplies with each passing year. This is evident by the number of people falling through the gaping cracks of our socioeconomic system. Bloomberg Businessweek, celebrating that "things didn't get worse," reported that for the past 50 years "the percent of Americans living below the poverty line has increased each year, from 12.3 percent in 2006 to 15.1 percent in 2010."[73] According to the most recent Census Bureau analysis, the official poverty rate essentially held at 15 percent, meaning that 46.2 million people live below the poverty line.

Is it any coincidence that US suicide rates have risen sharply since the economic crisis began in 2007? According to data from the US Centers for Disease Control and Prevention, suicide rates have more than quadrupled from 2008 to 2010. "In the run-up to the U.S. presidential election, President Obama and Mitt Romney are debating how best to spur economic recovery," wrote Aaron Reeves of Britain's University of Cambridge, who led the research, which was submitted to The Lancet medical journal. "Missing from this discussion is consideration of how to protect Americans' health during these hard times."[74]

---

71   Robert C. Lieberman, "Why the Rich Are Getting Richer," *Foreign Affairs,* January/February, 2011.

72   Jack Ewing, "Across the World, Leaders Brace for Discontent and Upheaval," *New York Times,* January 25, 2012.

73   Karen Weise, "Record U.S. Poverty Rate Holds as Inequality Grows," Bloomberg Businessweek, September 12, 2012.

74   "Americans' Suicide Rates Up Since Economic Crisis Began," Reuters, November 4, 2012.

At the same time, the US government is already smashed up against the deficit ceiling, yet nobody—least of all the rich corporations—wants to pay a fair share of the tax burden to at least feign a semblance of egalitarianism in the nation. Thus, state programs to assist the vulnerable segment of society get slashed or cancelled, while the too-big-to-fail banks and corporations receive a free lunch (as well as a convenient "get out of jail free" card for the next time they implode the economy). At the same time, Washington continues with its ill-advised overseas adventures, which the country can no longer afford. [75]

Given the extent of the economic gloom and doom, it might be expected that corporate America is also struggling in the aftermath of the worst economic crisis to hit America since the Great Depression. In fact, nothing could be further from the truth. While the US workforce is quietly suffering from soaring unemployment levels, alongside record productivity levels, corporate America is behaving as if it were business as usual. One reason corporations are breezing through the storm is due to America's extreme culture of deregulation. This hands-off approach to the so-called free market has become an unspoken rule of globalization, which demands that the transnational corporations be given total license in the never-ending quest for power and profits.

---

75 Arguing that the "members of the policy elite" are responsible for the present crisis now gripping the United States and much of the world, Paul Krugman pointed to the "Bush tax cuts, which added roughly $2 trillion to the national debt over the last decade. Second, there were the wars in Iraq and Afghanistan, which added an additional $1.1 trillion or so. And third was the Great Recession, which led both to a collapse in revenue," in the *New York Times*, "The Unwisdom of the Elites," May 8, 2011.

CHAPTER II
The Incredibly Shrinking American

The modern capitalist economic order is a huge universe into which the individual is born and in which he must live and which is for him, as an individual, given and unalterable.

—MAX WEBER, *THE PROTESTANT ETHIC AND THE SPIRIT OF CAPITALISM*

Once upon a time, American corporations performed their diverse functions according to the dictates of a state charter. In fact, the very founding of America was initiated by the London Company and the Plymouth Company—corporate entities that were granted royal charters by the king of England for the specific purpose of colonization and conquest. The beauty of the state charter was that it kept the unpredictable animal of the corporation on a tight leash. If any of these business entities failed to live up to its mandated duties, or became otherwise a public nuisance, they were relieved of their privileges *by the people.* Indeed, state-sanctioned charters were the closest thing we've ever had to real democratic control over these economic monstrosities. "State legislators maintained the sovereign right to withdraw the charter of any corporation that in their judgment failed to serve the public

41

interest" wrote David C. Korten, "and they kept close watch on corporate affairs."[76]

Today, corporations have a greater impact on our daily lives than any other institution, yet they are not bound by the rules of democratic procedure. We are able to vote our government leaders out of office if they fail to act on behalf of the public good, yet somehow corporations escape similar control. The reason is that these invasive entities are totally devoid of any internal restraint mechanism that serves to keep their power in check; the only democratic voice with any rights inside the corporate fortress belongs to that of the stockholders. But since the interests of this tiny group of individuals are directly diametrical to those of the people, they cannot be considered democratic as such.

Naturally, every business requires some breathing space to be a successful venture. Yet all too often corporate success comes at the expense of society, the environment, and, ironically, even the economy itself. The people are powerless to stop these transgressions. History has proved on numerous occasions that unlimited power naturally leads to unlimited abuses. "Constant experience shows us that every man invested with power is apt to abuse it, and to carry his authority as far as it will go," Montesquieu has written. "Is it strange, though true, to say that virtue itself has needs of limits? To prevent this abuse it is necessary from the very nature of things that *power should be checked by power*."[77]

The delightful irony of our plight is that corporations receive their awesome powers from "we the consumers" in the form of our daily purchases, as well as our hefty labor contributions. Thus, although it is rarely admitted, we all share a stake in the success and failure of the corporate world. Yet the people are only remembered (in the form of taxpayers) when it is time for yet another bailout of the too-big-to-fail banks and industries; we the people are considered malleable, expendable, and too powerless to worry about. Meanwhile, our business leaders, not content with merely dominating society and the economy at large, wish to assert them-

---

76   David C. Korten, *When Corporations Rule the World* (San Francisco: Kumarian Press, 1995), 57.

77   Montesquieu, *The Spirit of the Laws*, Book XI, Sec. 4.

selves in the one place they were never intended: the political domain. This is clearly stepping outside of acceptable boundaries. Corporations have turned the political arena into just another franchise that they control and manipulate at will. But since American society is structured in such a way that we are radically dependent upon corporations to provide our every need, fixing this problem will be no easy task. Before we take a stand against Monsters Inc. and expel them from the political process, we must trace the rise of corporate power to see exactly how these out-of-control institutions won their political liberties in the first place.

WELCOME TO DARTMOUTH COLLEGE

The first democratic levee to collapse before the deluge came in 1819 with the Dartmouth College case, which resulted in the corporation being removed from its public leash. In this landmark ruling, the state of New Hampshire sought to revoke a charter issued to Dartmouth College in the days before the United States had won its independence from the British crown. Although the case ostensibly dealt with the question of legal contracts, Chief Justice John Marshall included an all-encompassing definition of a corporation into his final decision that is stunning in its range and implications:

"A corporation is an artificial being, invisible, intangible, and existing only in the contemplation of the law. Being a mere creature of law, it possesses only those properties which the charter of its creation confers upon it either expressly or as incidental to its very existence. These are such as are supposed best calculated to effect the object for which it was created. Among the more important are immortality, and, if the expression may be allowed, individuality; properties by which a perpetual succession of many persons are considered as the same, and may act as a single individual. They enable a corporation to manage its own affairs, and to hold property without the perplexing intricacies, the hazardous and endless necessity, of perpetual conveyances for the purpose of transmitting it from hand to hand."

In one sweeping sleight of hand, the wolf of the corporation was granted access of our public parks, albeit in sheep's clothing. Indeed, upon further inspection it is difficult to say whether Marshall was formulating a definition of a corporation or God himself. In an incredible stretch of the legal imagination, the heavenly ordained human trait of individuality has been grafted upon the animal of the corporation.

Let us review, point by point, the *legal* definition of a multinational corporation as established in the Dartmouth College case. A corporation has been legally defined as:

1. An artificial being
2. Invisible, intangible, and existing only in the contemplation of the law
3. A mere creature of law
4. Immortal ("immortality")
5. An individual ("individuality")
6. [Defined by] properties by which a perpetual succession of many persons are considered as the same
7. [An entity that may] act as a single individual
8. [An entity that may] manage its own affairs
9. [An entity that may] hold property without the "perplexing intricacies"

Every one of the above lines is fraught with direct threats to our democracy. How is it possible that a very real organization, with very real attributes, could be deemed an "artificial" entity? What exactly did Judge Marshall mean when he described the tangible corporation as "invisible"? (The question is not simply a matter of semantics; the deliberate choice of words contained in this ruling is what has allowed for very liberal interpretations in later court cases.) Was it assumed that by deeming these business entities as artificial it would somehow serve to cloud the reality of corporate power? Furthermore, if this newly contrived beast of burden is really artificial, what or who is it pretending to be? Maybe just another harmless, "artificial" corporation?

What would be our natural reaction if we suddenly discovered that something we have been regularly feeding to our children, for example, in the belief that it was healthy and natural, turns out to be "artificial?" Our first impulse would be to find out what is really contained in the product masquerading as something it is not. We would painstakingly read the ingredients to determine, based on our limited knowledge of such things, if the produce is potentially harmful. Our need for answers concerning artificial products should be no different than it is concerning the "artificial corporation."

Labeling corporations as an "artificial being" gives them a cloak of invisibility that permits these entities to behave without fear of a public backlash. (Marshall may have been expressing the brutal political philosophy of Thomas Hobbes, the author of *Leviathan*, who argued that any collective body of individuals is merely artificial and will remain a "headless" multitude until legitimate representatives serve in the name of the group. And since the corporate universe is void of democratic avenues for its many participants, it may be argued that the corporation is indeed "artificial." But why should we permit anything to imitate through artifice and cunning the only true individuals—the proud, rugged individuals of the human variety?)

Equally unsettling, the corporation has been described as "invisible" as if it were some sort of comic book villain possessed of supernatural powers from a distant planet. Yet the consequences of corporate behavior—from environmental destruction, to political manipulation, to technological proliferation, to name just a few—cannot be considered "invisible." Indeed, corporate behavior is having a massive physical impact on all living beings and things. Is it possible to call the contamination of the Gulf of Mexico, for example, by a recent oil spill some sort of "invisible" consequence by an invisible entity? Is the unsustainable amount of waste and rubbish now polluting our environment "invisible?" Are the millions of people left unemployed in the wake of the latest economic crisis "invisible?" Certainly not. Corporations are no more "invisible" than the physical consequences of their increasingly egregious, destructive behavior.

Moving on, in lines II and III, we find that the vast powers that have been turned over to the corporation are diminished by suggesting that they exist "only in the contemplation of the law," or that it is "a mere creature of the law." But in America, as in any other civilized society, no individual is above the law; the verdict of the court stands supreme. Therefore, to include the words "only" and "mere" in regards to the law seems to be an attempt to conceal the very real and disruptive powers that have been handed over to the corporate entities. In fact, it could almost be perceived as an attempt at public deception.

Further on, it is argued that the corporation has achieved (merely?) "immortality." Needless to say, to award such a designation to a faceless organization is deeply disturbing. How is it possible that the United States of America, a nation that long ago declared its loyalty to no power higher than the almighty God ("In God We Trust"), could sacrifice to the corporation the one attribute—*immortality*—that separates us mere mortals from God himself? This is little more than creating a radical new monarchy, complete with the powers of heredity, while denying the heavenly kingdom its secular role of a heaven-sanctioned throne. At least the medieval dynasties had the prudence and humility to submit their secular rule to the heavenly authority of the pope and the Almighty. Corporate power, according to Judge Marshall's definition, has no other master than itself.

Finally, the Dartmouth verdict concludes that the corporation, *despite* being *"artificial, invisible, intangible and existing only in the contemplation of the law,"* as well as possessing "immortality," is now a veritable "individual" as well. This part of Marshall's verdict represents the most devastating impact that the Dartmouth College case has had on American rugged individualism: "Being a mere creature of the law, [the corporation] possesses...immortality, and, if the expression may be allowed, individuality; properties by which a perpetual succession of many persons are considered as the same, and may act as a single individual."

With all due respect, Judge Marshall, the expression may not be allowed. After all, how can we hold out hope for "rugged individualism" and self-autonomy when corporations have been declared "artificial, invisible and immortal."? This devastating court ruling, and many others that would follow, has dramatically decreased the chances of millions of Americans achieving the elusive American Dream. In fact, it could even be argued that the individual (the human variant, that is, as opposed to the radical new individual of the corporation) no longer truly exists, has been made completely irrelevant, for when in competition with such manifested powers, above and beyond those of any mortal being, the human spirit must wither and die.

In a pluralistically conceived democracy, which is devised to be governed and guided by the "general will" of our many diverse participants, it is impossible to compete against the *collective* force of the mega-wealthy corporate world. Individualism is a sacred human gift; to attribute this constitutional value to the corporation is nothing short of treachery. Thus, it would be no exaggeration to say that the Dartmouth College case is to corporate power what the Communist Manifesto was for the communists. But this case was only the first step in a steadily evolving betrayal of American individualism and autonomy.

CORPORATIONS ACHIEVE PERSONHOOD

In 1886, the US Supreme Court went one step further in empowering the corporations in the *Santa Clara County v. Southern Pacific Railroad* case, where it was decided that private corporations are entitled to the rights found in the Fourteenth Amendment. (Section 1 of that amendment declares that *"All persons born or naturalized in the United States, and subject to the jurisdiction thereof, are citizens of the United States and of the State wherein they reside. No State shall make any law which shall abridge the privileges or immunities of citizens of the United States; nor shall any State deprive any person of life, liberty, or property, without due process of law; nor deny to any person within its jurisdiction the equal protection of the law."*)

It is important to remember that the Fourteenth Amendment was brought into force to promote the well-being of

African Americans, Native Americans, and individuals born on US soil to foreign-born nationals. No mention was ever made to corporations in the US Constitution for one simple reason: Our Founding Fathers had no wish to grant these economic entities such broad powers, nor was such an outrageous notion ever conceived. Yet with one bang of the courtroom gavel, corporations acquired "personhood," which gave these business establishments all the rights and privileges originally reserved for American citizens.

The Supreme Court ruled in this case that "the words 'person' and 'whoever' include corporations, companies, associations, firms, partnerships, societies, and joint stock companies, as well as individuals." The problem with the Santa Clara County case, however, is that it was based upon pure fraud and deception. The question as to whether or not a corporation could be considered a legal person was never actually determined, at least not in a fair and legal manner. That is because the court reporter in the case, Bancroft Davis, attached a devastating comment into the headnote of the case summary long after the case was closed. Davis wrote: "The defendant Corporations are persons within the intent of the clause in section 1 of the Fourteenth Amendment to the Constitution of the United States, which forbids a State to deny any person within its jurisdiction the equal protection of the laws....The court does not wish to hear argument on the question whether the provision in the Fourteenth Amendment to the Constitution, which forbids a State to deny to any person within its jurisdiction the equal protection of the laws, applies to the corporations. *We are all of the opinion that it does.*" (Italics added.)

The story gets better, however, because Bancroft Davis was no mere court reporter. In fact, he had previously served as the president of the Newburgh and New York Railway Company. Should we chalk it up to the muse of coincidence that a former railroad president found himself in the position of court reporter in one of the most controversial court cases of all time, and one that involved, no less, a railroad? While Davis's headnote didn't carry the force of law, once the court quoted it in later decisions, the concept of corporate personhood magically became the law.[78]

So, in addition to the metaphysical powers (artificiality, immortality, individuality…) attributed to corporations in the Dartmouth College case, we must also wrangle with the fact that these business entities enjoy all the protection originally designed for "the people" (that is, of the mortal, flesh and blood variety) in the Fourteenth Amendment. At this point, we may be forgiven for wondering if our greatest historical document was really intended to open with "We the Corporations…" as opposed to "We the People."

What has come to pass is that the corporation, emboldened by its financial clout, political proximity, and global influence, is a legally ordained individual just like any human being. Yet contained inside the belly of this "individual" are millions of other individuals (that is, "We the People"), which have no choice but to support corporate power through their labor pains and consumer spending. Indeed, without the people, corporations would be weak, powerless creatures, while the same could not be said the other way around. If corporations were to suddenly disappear, or fall under democratic oversight, the people would immediately recover their lost autonomy and independence, and our neighborhoods would become brighter, more liveable places overnight. Sadly, this is not about to happen anytime soon. "The single separate citizen has no longer the power and independence that he had in Locke's speculations," lamented Bertrand Russell. "Our age is one of organization, and its conflicts are between organizations, not between separate individuals."[79] The problem with considering bloodless corporations to be people has tremendous moral implications as well. Noam Chomsky observed that "corporations were given the rights of immortal persons, but special kinds of persons—persons who had no moral conscience. You expect a human being to care about others but corporations are

---

78   See Thom Hartmann, *Unequal Protection: The Rise of Corporate Dominance and the Theft of Human Rights* (Rodale Press, 2004).
79   Russell, *History of Western Philosophy*, 582.

designed by law to be concerned only with the financial interests of its stockholders."[80]

Meanwhile, with corporate power now dominating every area of our lives, the whole notion of "fair competition"—and not just in the realm of economics—has been taken to a radical new playing field and beyond the reach of most mortals. Although we now share all of the same legal rights with corporations, human beings are permanently rooted in the local; we do not have the physical resources or global reach to compete with the economic and political clout of the globetrotting transnational corporations. Indeed, instead of competing with like-minded entrepreneurs on a level playing field, we are painfully dependent upon corporations to supply all of our needs and wants—from the basic essentials required for our survival, to the superfluous luxury items. From start to finish, we have lost the independence once associated with the fiercely proud rugged individual. Meanwhile, the myth of an "endless frontier" was officially closed over a century ago. It will require a social awakening before we can hope to free ourselves from this extreme dependency.

In his annual address to Congress, President Grover Cleveland summarized the challenge confronting the nation: "As we view the achievements of aggregated capital, we discover the existence of trusts, combinations, and monopolies, while the citizen is struggling far in the rear or is trampled to death beneath an iron heel. Corporations, which should be the carefully restrained creatures of the law and the servants of the people, are fast becoming the people's masters."[81]

CORPORATIONS WIN POLITICAL VOICE

Once corporations had acquired all of the legal rights and privileges that had been reserved explicitly for the people, it was only natural that they would take advantage of the designation for

---

80   Noam Chomsky interview in *The Corporation*, a documentary film by Mark Achbar, Jennifer Abbott, and Joel Bakan. http://www.thecorporation.com, 2004.
81   Grover Cleveland, quoted in Thom Hartmann, *Unequal Protection*, at http://www.commondreams.org/views03/0101–07.

increasing their grip on political and economic power. This came with the Supreme Court case *First National Bank of Boston v. Bellotti* (1978), when it was ruled that corporations have First Amendment rights to the freedom of speech. This decision opened the floodgates of Congress to the corporate lobbyists, turning the representatives of the people into custodians of the corporate purse. And since the people cannot hope to compete with corporate "freedom of speech," which is based on the simple arithmetic of hard cash, our politicians have become de facto servants of corporate interests.

Our political leaders failed to heed the sound counsel of Justice William Rehnquist, one of the dissenting judges in *First National Bank of Boston v. Bellotti,* who observed that "restrictions upon the political activity of business corporations are both politically desirable and constitutionally permissible." Rehnquist reminded the court that corporations enjoyed the protection of their property since they had already been legally designated with corporate "personhood." Thus, there was no need for corporate lobbyists clogging up Congress, working on behalf of special interests.

"So long as the Judicial Branches of the State and Federal Governments remain open to protect the corporation's interest in its property, it has no need, though it may have the desire, to petition the political branches for similar protection," Rehnquist continued. "Indeed, the States might reasonably fear that the corporation would use its economic power to obtain further benefits beyond those already bestowed."

The consequences of corporate power indulging our representatives with cash became most conspicuous at the height of the economic crisis. With families struggling to make the monthly rent, a veritable army of insurance company lobbyists was ascending on Congress in an effort to block health care reform. A report compiled by the *Financial Times* quoted statistics by the Center for Responsive Politics: "[B]y the end of 2009, the sums spent lobbying lawmakers on healthcare and insurance reform—roughly $430m—outpaced lobbying on any issue in the history of Congress. Indeed, total lobbying figures for 2009 increased by

5 percent year-on-year to an unprecedented \$3.47 bn."[82] Health care reform was simply meant to give all American people a fair chance of receiving affordable drugs and medical treatment. The health care industry, together with its lobbyists, made sure that that did not happen.

In the end, the American people got a watered-down version of health care reform, leaving all the power in the hands of the health industry corporations and insurance companies. But the bloodsuckers inside corporate America were still not satisfied. Before the health care legislation had barely passed Obama's desk, it received a major setback when twenty-nine firms, representing nearly one million US employees, fought and got health care coverage waivers after threatening to ax coverage for their employees altogether. Naturally, instead of calling corporate America's bluff and letting the people judge for themselves these deplorable actions, the government backed down. "Nearly a million workers won't get a consumer protection in the U.S. health reform law meant to cap insurance costs because the government exempted their employers," reported *USA Today*. "Thirty companies, including McDonald's and Jack in the Box, won't be required to raise the minimum annual benefit included in low-cost health plans, which are often used to cover part-time and low-wage employees." The report added that the companies forced the government waivers after threatening to "drop health insurance altogether."[83] Without any sort of public debate, corporate America bent the arm of the White House backward and got its way. So much for health care reform.

What lessons has this form of indentured servitude taught our political representatives, who are supposed to be fighting on behalf of the public interest? They learned—if they did not know it already—that the real money is not to be made while serving in government, but rather in working as a corporate lobbyist on Capitol Hill. Today, there is a well-greased revolving door between Capitol Hill and Wall Street that allows retiring members of Con-

---

82   Stephanie Kirchgaessner, "Under the Influence," *Financial Times*, March 16, 2010.
83   Drew Armstrong, "McDonald's, 29 Other Firms Get Health Care Coverage Waivers," *USA Today*, October 11, 2010.

gress, who earn a measly $174,000 a year in Congress, to more than triple their income as corporate lobbyists.

The choice for our government representatives, in the face of rich temptations and huge campaign donations, has largely become one between the pluralist demands of the people—Rousseau's "general will"—and the lobbying power of corporations and foreign nations.[84] Thus, the very fact that our politicians must choose between their own people on the one hand and huge conglomerations of economic wealth on the other is at once the very essence of the problem. There was never intended to be any external competition in the halls of government, or on the main streets of civilized communities, when the issue at stake was the very representation of the people, by the people and for the people. Those who hold power within the halls of government have forgotten that "the state becomes a reality only when it corresponds to the given potentialities of men and permits their full development."[85]

Public Citizen, a Washington-based watchdog group, recently asked forty-seven members in the House and Senate if they would be willing to sign a pledge not to accept a job with a lobbying firm upon retirement. Not one of the lawmakers took the challenge, and that should not be too surprising considering the track record. According to Public Citizen, at least seventy former members of Congress were employed in 2009 as lobbyists for the financial services sector alone.[86] The damage that this partnership has done to our democratic heritage is incalculable. After all, how many of our representatives in Congress are going to jeopardize a lucrative future job with some corporation upon retirement by pushing them too hard while in office? Indeed, it opens the door to speculation that compliant congressmen are being secretly

---

84   Former Speaker of the House Robert Livingston resigned from office in 1999 and founded the Livingston Group, one of the most influential and powerful lobbies on Capitol Hill, which comprises a powerful network of over forty principals, consultants, and international associates, including former congressional members of both major parties, former members of political staffs, and corporate executives.

85   Herbert Marcuse, *Reason and Revolution* (London: Rutledge, 1986), 2nd Ed. 11.

86   Arthur Delaney, "Lawmakers Ignore Call to Promise Not to Become Lobbyists," *Huffington Post*, April 21, 2010.

offered future positions as lobbyists on the condition that such-and-such piece of legislation is accepted or axed.

Thus, it is easy to understand why, with corporations now able to buy the political platform of choice, the move for campaign reform is going nowhere: Very few politicians, regardless of their stance on the issue, can afford alienating the corporate paymasters. After all, it is never a problem finding politicians who are willing to sell their political soul to the highest bidder. In fact, such behavior today is considered absolutely normal. This perverted form of "democratic representation," which allows our government officials to become subservient to the highest bidders, has corrupted our political system to the bone; gangrene has set in, and the only thing left to do is amputate. After all, there is a very limited amount of political representation available, both in terms of time and energy, which our politicians are able to dedicate to their voters. Yet the overwhelming majority of a politician's term in office is spent defending the rights of big business. And why should it be otherwise when it is the corporations that are pumping the most money into the electoral process?

CITIZENS DISUNITED

The consequences of allowing corporations to masquerade as living, breathing persons has allowed these economic monstrosities to become firmly entrenched in our political system—the one place that corporate interests were never intended or designed to be. And like a snowball that picks up more speed and volume as it moves downhill, the same thing is happening in regards to corporate power. It is snowballing to such great dimensions that nobody, it seems, is in the position to block its outrageous demands. Thus, we should not have been surprised when the Republican-leaning majority in the US Supreme Court ruled in *Citizens United v. Federal Election Commission (2010)*, that transnational corporations may spend unlimited amounts of cash financing local and national elections. This watershed case, which ignored many years of sound, conservative counsel that guarded our nation against the hazards of mixing business and politics, has opened the floodgates on corporate spending, turning our already compromised election process into a corporate-sponsored carnival.

The highly controversial Citizens United ruling gives both domestic and foreign corporations the unlimited "freedom of speech" to bankroll the political platform of their choice. Yet these shady new players are under no obligations to make public disclosures of their donations. In other words, corporations have gained the "freedom of speech" to flood the political process with their dollars, but the public has no freedom to information as to where the campaign dollars are going, nor by whom. The five Republican-leaning justices proved that they understood exactly how disruptive their decision was by issuing a statement saying they were confident the people will not "lose faith in this democracy" due to the ruling, which sounds more of a warning than anything.

"Independent expenditures, including those made by corporations, do not give rise to corruption or the appearance of corruption," the five justices wrote in their fiercely subjective opinion. "[Just because] speakers may have influence over or access to elected officials does not mean that those officials are corrupt. And the appearance of influence or access will not cause the electorate to lose faith in this democracy." The sheer arrogance of that statement, which assumes to speak on behalf of the people on an intensely controversial issue, is simply astounding. More important, it represents a corporate coup d'état in the field of politics, essentially silencing the voice of the electorate, or at the very least making it redundant.

"How can five justices sweep aside what elected officials themselves long ago concluded on the subject and claim to know what will or will not 'cause the electorate to lose faith in this democracy,'" asked E. J. Dionne Jr. in the *Washington Post*. "Could anything undermine trust in the system more than secret contributions to shadowy groups spending the money on nasty ads?"[87]

---

87   E. J. Dionne Jr., "Shadowy Players in a New Class War," *Washington Post*, October 11, 2010.

On the upside of the decision, Dionne argued, is that "the class war is bringing...clarity to politics." If the specter of "class war" is now viewed as the positive side of this court case, then we really have wallowed into some deep and dangerous waters. If we can be forgiven for dragging Marxist terminology into the debate, "bourgeois capitalism" has not just separated the producer, i.e., the workers, from the means of production; capitalism has practically succeeded in separating the producers from their political voice, which is a far greater danger than the former.

Jamie Raskin, professor of law at American University and senator from Maryland, provided a shocking glimpse as to what extent corporate power may now intervene in our political system: "In 2008, the Fortune 100 corporations had $600 billion in profit. Now imagine if those top 100 companies decided to spend a modest 1 percent of their profits to intervene in politics and get their way. That would mean $6 billion, or double what the Obama campaign spent, the McCain campaign spent, and every candidate for the House and Senate."[88]

Senior Justice John Paul Stevens, one of the four dissenting justices in the Supreme Court case, rightly warned that *Citizens United* would introduce a flux of foreign cash by "nonresidents" under the guise of transnational corporations to manipulate the US political system. "*Corporations are not actually members of [our society]. They cannot vote or run for office. Because they may be managed and controlled by nonresidents, their interests may conflict in fundamental respects with the interests of eligible voters. The financial resources, legal structure, and instrumental orientation of corporations raise legitimate concerns about their role in the electoral process. Our lawmakers have a compelling constitutional basis, if not also a democratic duty, to take measures designed to guard against the potentially deleterious effects of corporate spending in local and national races.*"

Today, lobbyists indulge our political representatives with an amount of campaign contributions, gifts, and even bribes that can never be fully exposed through investigation. As the *Financial Times*

---

88   Comments from www.FreeSpeechForPeople.org Youtube title "FreeSpeechForPeople.org."

reported on the latest US presidential elections, "The US presidential candidates are heading towards the $1bn mark in campaign fundraising, shattering records as Wall Street and corporate America pump cash into a race that started early....The highly competitive field has forced corporations to generously spread their contributions to ensure continued good standing with potential future presidents."[89]

Meanwhile, individuals who enter political office without outstanding debts to the corporate masters are branded as eccentrics who are not to be taken seriously. "Dark horse" political candidates such as Ross Perot, Steve Forbes, and Donald Trump—individuals who are in the financial position to foot the bill for their own campaigns—fail to reach office precisely because they had no need for corporate sponsorship and therefore debts to repay in the form of political favors once in office. The media label such individuals as "unpredictable."

CORPORATIONS ENTHRONED

Due to these and other uncontested court cases, corporations now dominate the last avenue of power in American politics, which separates free and autonomous men from the oppressed. That is, of course, his democratic representation. As we can clearly see, corporate political spending is out of proportion to their representational powers; these economic behemoths do not represent the American people, do not defend the American peoples' interests on any single issue, yet they want to control the course of our political river. It's absurd.

Meanwhile, Judge Marshall, who presided over the Dartmouth College case, was even thoughtful enough to relieve corporations from the "perplexing intricacies" of managing its own affairs. What

89   Ben White, "Race to Become $1 bn President," the *Financial Times*, February 1, 2008, 10. It cannot be ignored that Citizens United was passed by a Republican-leaning Supreme Court in the same year that the Republicans were looking to take command again of Congress by winning the midterm elections—which they handily did thanks in large part to record campaign spending. The Supreme Court was designed to be an impartial mediator in the most crucial issues facing the nation. With the passage of Citizens United, it is obvious this is no longer the case.

hardworking American would ever stoop so low and demand such a pathetic guarantee? Clearly, corporations are demanding a free ride from the government and American taxpayer, an attitude that has much more in common with socialism than capitalism. And if things continue as they have been, we may live to see the day when a corporation decides to make a run for political office.

Meanwhile, there seems to be some "political justice" occurring inside the Supreme Court over the wisdom of its long tradition of business-friendly decisions. Just five months after passing its calamitous ruling on corporate spending in state and national campaigns, it was announced as part of a "security overhaul" that the public would no longer pass through the iconic bronze doors, designed by architect Cass Gilbert, when entering the seventy-five-year-old Supreme Court building. As several justices observed, the public's right to enter the highest court in the land was a metaphor for "access to the court itself."

"The significance of the court's front entrance extends beyond its design and function," Justice Stephen G. Breyer wrote in a statement joined by Justice Ruth Bader Ginsburg. "Writers and artists regularly use the steps to represent the ideal that anyone in this country may obtain meaningful justice through application to this Court....In short, time has proven the success of Gilbert's vision: To many members of the public, this court's main entrance and front steps are not only a means to, but also a metaphor for, access to the court itself." Today, "access to the court itself" is increasingly the privilege of corporate interests alone; tragically, the American rugged individual is becoming an anomaly in his own country.

As one of America's wisest leaders foresaw many years ago, there can be just one possible outcome for a system that allows the "money power" to invade our fragile political space. "Corporations have been enthroned," President Abraham Lincoln observed shortly before his untimely death. "An era of corruption in high places will follow and the money power will endeavor to prolong its reign by working on the prejudices of the people...until wealth is aggregated in a few hands...and the Republic is destroyed."[90]

---

90   As quoted in Harvey Wasserman, *America Born & Reborn* (New York: Collier Books, 1983), 89–90.

AMERICA'S RUGGED INDIVIDUAL: AN ENDANGERED SPECIES

individualism *n* **1**: EGOISM **2**: a doctrine that the interests of the individual are primary **3**: a doctrine holding that the individual has political or economic rights which the state must not interfere.[91]

Since the founding of America, the individual has been heralded as the ultimate master of his destiny and the hero of history. The philosophy of "rugged individualism"—a term coined by Alexis de Tocqueville during his famous nineteenth-century American tour—expressed what was deep in the heart and soul of every American: a longing for individual pursuit and initiative irrespective of the dangers involved. Armed with little more than their God-given fortitude and determination, Americans were confident the myriad challenges of the New World would be conquered. As James Bryce, a former British ambassador to the United States (1907–13), observed, "Individualism, the love of enterprise, and the pride in personal freedom have been deemed by Americans not only their choicest, but [their] peculiar and exclusive possession."[92]

Given this fierce dedication to independence, it should come as no surprise that Americans remain estranged from their government. This is a vestige of the pioneer days and the cowboy experience when rugged individualism mingled warily with interdependence, as towns and villages seemed to arise more for protective purposes than from any desire for men to live in close proximity to one another. Government, always viewed with an excessive amount of fear and loathing by the pioneers, was duly accepted as a necessary evil. "I heartily accept the motto," Henry David Thoreau famously declared, "that government is best which governs least."[93]

In the early days of American history, it was the strength and vitality of great men—names like Washington, Franklin, Crockett,

---

91   *New Merriam-Webster's Dictionary* (Springfield, Massachusetts, 1989).
92   James Bryce, *The American Commonwealth*, 1888.
93   Henry David Thoreau, *On the Duty of Civil Disobedience*, 1847, 1.

and Thoreau—who personified the concept of rugged individualism. Through the rare gift of a vast and seemingly unconquerable frontier, these men, and many others like them, were blessed with the once-in-a-lifetime opportunity for staking out their own private, autonomous domain while pledging allegiance not only to their nation, but to their self-autonomy as well. Over time, however, the tremendous challenges facing the young nation allowed publicly chartered corporations to increasingly oversee many of the big projects, which included the construction of the railroads and factory system. Unfortunately, Americans were unable to foresee the rise of corporate power that would eventually rise out of the smoke and filth of the industrial age. "Here we clung to the credo of 'rugged individualism' long after the individual had been hopelessly overwhelmed by the environment of massive industrialism," noted Robert L. Heilbroner, American economist and historian.[94]

Max Weber, the German sociologist, pointed to stringent Puritan ethics and ideas, which idealized a life of toil and labor, as providing the necessary tools for the rise of America's peculiar form of capitalism. The gritty reality behind the "spirit of capitalism," however, goes far in explaining why Americans persevere in the face of unbearable adversity and march on like good Christian soldiers despite intolerable conditions. "Protestant individualism," wrote Isaiah Berlin, "as the 'ideological' counterpart of...trade and production, taught men to believe that the individual held the means for his happiness in his own hands, that faith and energy were sufficient to secure it."[95] For the economic elite in America, any governmental handouts that do not directly assist their own privileged class is attacked as yet another step toward socialism. Never mind that the banks and corporations are not ashamed to stand in line at the community soup kitchen for their free government handouts, which are heavily subsidized by middle-class tax money.

Paradoxically, the fierce individualism that the American people have come to cherish is the reason we are failing to unite

---

94   Robert Heilbroner, *The Worldly Philosophers* (New York: Touchstone, 1999), 168.
95   Berlin, *Karl Marx*, 109.

against the consolidated threat of corporate power at this crucial hour. We complain about excessive government intrusiveness in our lives, yet we silently accept the overarching reign of corporate power, which is proving to be the far greater menace. This is what has made our blind dedication to individualism so potentially perilous: It demands, almost as dogma, that every individual fend completely for himself in the social, economic, and political realms. Indeed, it is almost as if an individual's personal success was directly proportional to the beneficence of the Almighty. The failure to achieve success is due to an individual's personal failings and shortcomings as opposed to an unfair playing field, and the slew of "self-help" books on the market would seem to prove that point. "Every man had it in his power to attain to spiritual or material well-being," Berlin continues, "that for his weakness and misery he ultimately had only himself to blame."

While we cling to the credo of rugged individualism, telling ourselves that it is honorable to pursue our life goals without outside help, the largest economic organizations are free to merge together and seek government assistance. Indeed, as already noted, corporate lobbyists spend prodigious sums of money securing the representation of our political leaders, while watering down important public programs, like health care and education. Afraid of being branded "communists" by uniting together against corporate power, the American people—each one in his or her own silent way—is suffering undue economic and political oppression under the iron heel of this system. Indeed, adhering to the otherwise brave philosophy of rugged individualism at this critical juncture gives corporations the ability to manipulate this brittle aggregate—the classic strategy of divide and conquer—for its own wealth, power, and prosperity. "The failure of an economy to generate rising incomes for a majority over decades causes frustration," admitted Martin Wolf, a columnist with the *Financial Times*. "US individualism may contain this reaction. Most cultures cannot."[96]

---

96   Martin Wolf, "The Rich Rewards and Poor Prospects of a New Gilded Age," Financial Times, April 26, 2006, 11. In this column, Wolf cites a "remarkable paper" from two economists at Northwestern University who ask a simple but telling question: "If the US economy

It must be stressed lest we are misunderstood: Rugged individualism is not something to be shunned or ashamed of. On the contrary, our rugged individualism is a wholly unique American trait that is to be guarded and nurtured. But we must also be clear as to the reality of our historical situation: We are not living in days of Henry David Thoreau, and there is no more untamed frontier to escape to when things get rough. In light of our brave new world, retreating into the shell of rugged individualism will not save us; indeed, falling back on this philosophy will only worsen our situation. The philosophy of rugged individualism was inspired by the unique experience our ancestors faced while settling our once wild, savage land. Those days are over, yet the instinct to remain a solitary rugged individual continues. It is a courageous stance, but ultimately a suicidal one. The problem with following the creed of individualism is that other individuals will not hesitate to take advantage of our divisive, self-obsessed state of mind to advance their own individual agenda. "One-tenth of humanity will have the right to individuality and will exercise unlimited authority over the other nine-tenths," wrote Albert Camus. "The latter will lose their individuality and become like a flock of sheep."[97]

Instead of individualism, what the American people desperately need today is a group awakening to confront the threats looming on the horizon. As long as there exist collective forces of economic power, there must be an equally powerful collective force to balance the scales. Currently, this is not the case, which explains the atmosphere of corruption and abuse of power now commonplace throughout the US business community. It also explains the rise of protest movements across the United States and across the political spectrum. The American people are being pulled between the two most entrenched ideologies: laissez-faire economics, which is largely a battlefield reserved for the transnational corporations, and rugged individualism, where the average man relies on nothing more than his own personal resources for his survival and success.

While it is admirable to want to live an individualistic lifestyle, as a freedom-loving individual, it quickly becomes a huge liability

---

is becoming more productive, why have most of its citizens not become better off?" Is the answer connected to corporate America's lack of "corporate democracy" within its walls?

97   Albert Camus, *The Rebel* (London: Penguin Books, 1951), 144.

if there are members in that society who may be tempted to take advantage of that lonely status for personal and private gain. To better understand the inherent weakness of the individual, and the inherent threats the philosophy entails, consider this parable handed down to us from antiquity: "The Scythian fathers thought, with good reason, that they left their children a valuable inheritance, when they left them in peace and union with one another. One of their kings, whose name was Scylurus, finding himself draw near his end, sent for all his children, and giving to each of them one after another a bundle of arrows tied fast together, desired them to break them. Each used his endeavours, but was not able to do it. Then untying the bundle, and giving them the arrows one by one, they were very easily broken. Let this image, says the father, be a lesson to you of the mighty advantage that results from union and concord."[98] Scylurus's descendants proved to be excellent students, for soon thereafter they found themselves under attack from the Persian king, Darius. But the Scythians, thanks to the lesson they had received on "union and concord" did not break in the face of a challenge by a more powerful army. Eventually, the Persians gave up their plans for conquest and returned home.

Until we understand that man is no longer the central character in the great game of life, but a mere spectator to massive conglomerates vying for ultimate power, we will continue to languish under the boot of collective corporate power. When men and women agree to compete in the economic arena according to the rules of globalization (indeed, do we have any choice?) their competition is not merely against other rugged individuals of the human variety. Our main competitor has become the very rugged individual of corporate power—a force that has pushed the average citizen and entrepreneur completely off the human stage. As one scholar described the situation, the present economic paradigm is responsible for "individualizing and fragmenting, reducing to zero all forms of resistance."[99] Indeed, our fierce individualism, compounded by

---

98   Charles Rollins, *Ancient History* (Boston: Samuel Walker, 1823), vol.1, 259.
99   Ian R. Douglas, *Globalization and the Retreat of the State*, adapted from *Globalization and the Politics of Resistance*, International Political Economy Series, edited by Barry K. Gills, (England: Palgrave, 2000), 127.

the well-documented "loneliness of modern man" in impersonal urban surroundings, breaks down the natural bonds between people to the point where parents cannot even enjoy a truly meaningful relationship with their children, let alone assemble in just cause with their fellow men.

As was already outlined in the previous chapter, corporations themselves have been decreed as legal individuals. So the question remains: How do we take on corporate power as proud individuals without losing our basic freedoms in the process? The way to square this circle of taming corporate power is to allow for more democracy, not less, inside the corporate fortress. Predictably, corporate power will be fighting against such a "radical" proposal behind closed doors, and this betrays its anti-democratic credentials from the start. Such a call to action must have the strong support of our government representatives, which won't be easy given their craven devotion to their corporate paymasters.

In the not-so-distant past, when corporate power was still in its infancy, our political representatives were more sensitive to the demands of their constituents. If the citizen was the lightning bolt, our government representatives were the lightning rod; in other words, the halls of power responded to the will of the people, and the community thrived because of it. This proud standing of the individual, a primary prerequisite of any democracy, no less for an economy, has been largely vanquished. It is time to reclaim what is rightfully ours.

Speaking on Alexis de Tocqueville's views American corporate power, R. Jeffrey Lustig wrote: "The associational life that impressed (de Tocqueville) was not that of the business corporation….What most impressed him were the town councils by which the New England townships governed themselves."[100] Such councils, he wrote with exaggerated optimism, would prevent further "centralization and atomization." Unfortunately for us, Tocqueville's worst fears about power and influence being concentrated into a few hands have been realized. Instead of protecting civil society from overwhelming external powers, we dropped our collective guard, Ralph Miliband argued long ago, allowing business enterprises to trample

---

100 Lustig, *Corporate Liberalism*, 133.

on our freedoms and rights in order to achieve the "highest possible profits for their own enterprises," which subordinates all other considerations, "including the public welfare."[101] While at one time the feared "individual" was a feudal lord, the church, or king, the menace of these modern times is the corporation.

Today, the corporation has displaced man from his central sphere of influence, which was the town center. Along Main Street, the individual played a truly purposeful role in his society as an entrepreneur, citizen, participant in the political process, and family man. The political, social, cultural, and economic identity of man was firmly established; man was complete, so to speak. His voice, everyman's most important possession, was loud enough within the social realm to be carried to all corners of his society.

"Human life in communities only becomes possible," wrote Sigmund Freud, "when a number of men unite together in strength superior to any single individual and remain united against all single individuals."[102] The father of modern psychoanalysis went on to say that this "substitution of the power of a united number for the power of a single man is the decisive step towards civilization." Freud described in a few succinct lines the entire history and essence of modern democracy, which has been the removal or containment of small, arbitrary factions in favor of the individual rights of man.

Throughout the course of human history, the American people have waged battles against powerful "individual" adversaries. Yet the war is still not finished. Those past tyrannies from which we freed ourselves are still very much with us, with one key exception: The costumes have changed. Today, the usurpers hide themselves behind the corporate logo to conceal their undemocratic agenda from much of the world. After all, who would ever suspect that the very organizations that supply so much material pleasures could be responsible, at the same time, for destroying our democratic heritage?

---

101   Ralph Miliband, *The State in Capitalist Society* (London: Quartet Books, 1987), 33.
102   Sigmund Freud, *Civilization and Its Discontents* (New York: Dover Publications, 1994), 26.

CHAPTER III
Corporate America's War on Workers

Nothing then is unchangeable but the inherent and inalienable rights of man.

— Thomas Jefferson

It is certainly one of the world's greatest paradoxes. Despite America's professed devotion to democratic procedure, all avenues to representation inside corporate America have been systematically blocked or eliminated. At the same time, corporations dominate not just the economic scene but the political process as well. Thus, the prospects for management and the workers resolving their grievances without any outside arbitration is a bit like the lions and the sheep sitting down in a pasture to discuss grazing rights. Although we are all familiar with the morals of Aesop's fables, we continue to place excessive faith in such impossible arrangements.

Today, the closest thing to democratic representation inside the corporate universe, aside from that awarded to a handful of stockholders who enjoy voting privileges, falls under the battered flag of the labor unions. "Given that the US has one of the lowest rates of union membership in the industrialized world," reported the *Financial Times* just as the crisis was erupting, "it is not the obvious place to find the future of organized labour. Only about 7.5 percent of private sector American employees are in a union... [O]ne has to search hard to find many service sector professionals in unions," the article continued, while mentioning the ability of US corporations to "exclude unions, as they are allowed to do."[103]

In 2012, the rate of union membership in the public sector plunged more than a full percentage point, from 37 to 35.9 percent of workers. In the private sector, membership dropped from 6.9 to 6.6 percent. Meanwhile, the total number of Americans represented by a union 'stands' at 11.3 percent, down from 11.8 the previous year. This is the lowest rate since Uncle Sam began collecting data in 1983 – when the rate was about 35 percent. The battle cry heard today among members of the workforce has been reduced to: "We are so fortunate to still have our jobs!" Under the constant threat of ending up in the unemployment line, it is understandable why so many American workers are hesitant to stand up for their basic human rights. But there are some brave exceptions out there.

AMERICA'S UNSUNG HEROES

In the dead heat of the global economic downturn, when most people were terrified of joining the ranks of the unemployed, one man severed ties with his employer in dramatic fashion. As the story goes, Steven Slater, a former flight attendant with JetBlue, got involved in an argument with a passenger on a domestic flight as the plane was preparing for takeoff. In the ensuing confusion, Slater received a knock on the head from an overhead storage bin. Apparently, that was one knock too many for the JetBlue employee. Slater, however, decided he would go out in memorable fashion: When the plane came to a halt on the runway, he

---

103 John Gapper, "Workers of the New World Unite!" *Financial Times*, December 13, 2007, 11.

uttered a profanity-laced tirade over the aircraft's intercom system, grabbed a couple of cold beers from the refrigerator, and jumped ship by activating the plane's emergency escape slide. The FBI took Slater into custody—according to reports, in an overly aggressive manner—later that day.

Overnight, Steven Slater, who quite literally jumped ship without the benefit of a golden parachute now available to top executives, became a working-class hero with his unorthodox departure from the ranks of corporate America. After all, Slater had the nerve to say "take this job and shove it"—something most of us have dreamed about doing at least once in our working lives. The sudden national outpouring of support and sympathy for this one individual's act—reckless as it may have been—attests to the growing level of dissatisfaction being felt by millions of workers across the corporate universe.

"It's part of the frustration all over the country as employees take pay cuts and have to do double the workload as they take on the responsibilities of their laid-off co-workers," wrote Joanna Molloy in the *New York Daily News*. "I'm surprised it doesn't happen more often, but you gotta eat."[104] Suddenly, the corporate world was forced to sit up and take notice, as a slew of introspective articles on management style and worker relations suddenly came out of the woodwork, including this gem from *Forbes* magazine: "Airline employees and passengers aren't the only stressed-out folks these days," wrote Scott Spreier. "The economic crisis has created a level of ongoing stress and uncertainty that few of us ever experienced before, and many people, including very good people, are behaving very badly."[105]

Spreier then identified four steps for dealing with employee "outbursts": It is important to "take a deep breath" and make sure the "victim" is using the "rational part of his brain" so that he can "hear what you're saying," which will give you the opportunity to "seek the other person's cooperation." The article suggests what to do after an employee has demonstrated signs of

---

104 Joanna Molloy, "Take This Job and Shove It! JetBlue Flight Attendant Steven Slater Does What We All Dream of Doing," *New York Daily News*, September 3, 2010.
105 Scott Spreier, "How to Head Off the Steven Slater in Your Organization," *Forbes*, August 19, 2010.

"fatigue," as opposed to suggesting preventive measures that corporations might take (less enforced overtime, maybe?) to ensure that individuals are less prone to do something irrational in the first place. In other words, instead of corporations being proactive in their approach to the situation and introducing real reforms, they merely advise managers how to handle an employee who has already snapped. In other words, American workers must simply learn to cope with workplace stress, usually provoked by poor corporate work ethics.

To better appreciate the new challenges confronting working individuals everywhere, consider this brief excerpt from a leading business newspaper:

> Company Profits Soar
> NEW YORK – Profits at US
> companies soared 13.5 percent to a record $1.268.8bn in
> the final three months of 2004, boosted by strong demand
> and productivity growth coupled with workers' weak bargaining power.[106]

There you have it. The spate of profit taking alluded to in this brief yet loaded report was made possible due to the "workers' weak bargaining power," coupled with "strong demand and productivity growth." To put it another way, the US workforce must keep mental and physical pace with the endlessly evolving "money-saving technologies" that have helped to increase productivity rates—that is, the actual product the worker is creating per hour. Meanwhile, due largely to a fractured labor movement, workers no longer have the opportunity to negotiate for fair labor conditions and wages.

Judging by the grim picture inside corporate America, there are millions of Steven Slaters silently enduring untold hardships behind the walls of the corporate fortress. We just don't hear their stories because these individuals do not usually jump from aircraft when they decide to quit their jobs. To better appreci-

---

106 "Company Profits Soar," *Financial Times,* March 31, 2005.

ate how degraded US work conditions have become, let's take a deeper look at the airline industry, a microcosm of sorts for US labor conditions as a whole. The Bureau of Transportation Statistics reported the level of US airline employment in June 2010 was the second lowest in twenty years while annual passenger traffic surged 65 percent during the same period. Meanwhile, as the nation's top ten airlines generated around $8 billion in fees in 2009, while substituting hot meals for bags of peanuts, it is safe to say they are not hurting for cash or even customers.[107] Yet consideration for the airline industry's workers and their stretched-to-the-limit workloads continues to get third-class treatment. The tragic irony concerning the apparent stinginess of the airline companies is beginning to show a dangerous symptom: a string of fatigued air traffic controllers falling asleep at the radar screens, placing thousands of airline passengers at tremendous risk in increasingly crowded skies.

On March 23, 2011, two commercial airliners, carrying a total of 165 passengers, were forced to land at Reagan National Airport in Washington, DC, without guidance from the control tower after the sole air traffic controller fell asleep during the night shift. "As a former airline pilot, I am personally outraged that this controller did not meet his responsibility to help land these two airplanes," roared Randy Babbitt, Federal Aviation Administration chief.[108]

Although the air traffic controller was certainly at fault for dozing off on the job, little has been said about the FAA's responsibility of hiring enough individuals to ensure that such incidences do not happen in the first place. The harrowing incident forced regulators to add an additional controller on the midnight shift. But why were changes enforced only following a potentially catastrophic situation that could have resulted in the death of hundreds of people? This one example of corporate recklessness suggests rampant irresponsibility across the corporate world. After all, if the airline industry, which is under the

107 Carol Pucci, "Air Rage Soars as Airlines Cut Back," *Seattle Times*, August 12, 2010.
108 "'Sleeping' US Air Traffic Controller Suspended," BBC, March 24, 2011.

supervision of the federal government, fails to see that it is not employing enough people, imagine what the situation is like in the less-regulated sectors of the economy.

The incident at Reagan National Airport, however, was not an isolated event. In fact, the string of incidences at the beginning of 2011 points to an epidemic of gross negligence: In February 2011, an air traffic controller was found asleep on the job during the midnight shift at McGhee Tyson Airport in Knoxville, Tennessee; on March 29, two controllers at Preston Smith International Airport were suspended when they failed to hand off control of an aircraft and could not be reached by other controllers; on April 11, a controller at Seattle's Boeing Field-King County International Airport dozed off during the morning shift; finally, federal transportation officials were forced to intervene when an air ambulance carrying a critically ill patient was forced to land without guidance from a sleeping air traffic controller at Reno-Tahoe International Airport on April 13.[109]

The irony of these incidences, which luckily never resulted in disaster, is that wealthy corporate executives make up a large proportion of airline passenger traffic, yet they willingly put their own lives at risk by cutting off the branch—or in this case, the wing— they are sitting on by understaffing critical sectors of the economy. "Several large industries, including trucking, airlines, telecommunications, and others, have been deregulated, often at a substantial cost to their workers," a report by the Center for Economic and Policy Research (CEPR) revealed. "Many jobs in state and local government have been privatized and outsourced."[110] The report also had little positive news for college graduates: At every age level, "workers with four years or more of college are actually less likely to have a good job now than three decades ago." The researchers were startled by the findings because the US economy now has "almost twice as many workers with advanced degrees today as it did in 1979."

---

109 Keith Rogers, "FAA to Add More Controllers after Latest Sleeping Incident in Reno," *Las Vegas Review-Journal,* April 13, 2011.
110 John Schmitt and Janelle Jones, "Where Have All the Good Jobs Gone?," Center for Economic and Policy Research, July 2012, p. 1.

The conclusion of the CEPR report supports the thesis that there is a dearth of democracy inside of the corporate universe: "We believe…that the decline in the economy's ability to create good jobs is related to a deterioration in the bargaining power of workers."

PROFESSIONAL ATHLETES PAY THEIR DUES

Since union membership has plummeted to below 8 percent of the working population, long-term employment in any single sector of the economy has gone the way of chrome fenders and vinyl records as employers are increasingly relying on cheap part-time hires and temp agencies to fill the void.[111] At the same time, workers are reporting lower levels of job satisfaction than at any time in recent history.[112] Given these unsettling aspects of the modern workplace, it does not hurt to have a union behind you in the stormy season. This is something that even well-paid professional football players have come to appreciate.

Before the start of the National Football League's 2010-11 season-opening match, players for both the New Orleans Saints and Minnesota Vikings made a dramatic gesture that baffled observers. After the delivery of the national anthem, the members of both teams stepped forward simultaneously and extended their index fingers in a display of union solidarity. They would need it, because the players and the owners were on the brink of cancelling the season as negotiations for a new collective bargaining agreement [CBA] were stuck in the end zone. Saints quarterback Drew Brees, a member of the NFLPA executive board, said the planned gesture by both teams was coordinated to send a message

---

111 Reuters, "Manpower Beats Profits Forecasts Thanks to Demand for Short-Term Workers," October 20, 2010. The report points out that Manpower, the temp agency, posted "quarterly profits far ahead of Wall Street estimates…as it benefited from economic uncertainty in America."

112 According to a survey released in January 2009 by the Conference Board research group, just 45 percent of Americans said they are satisfied with their work. The survey, which looked at trends for 2008, was the lowest level ever recorded by the group in over two decades of studying the issue.

to the NFL that the players were united in their negotiations for a new contract. "Even though five minutes from then we were going to go out and bash each others' heads in," Brees told reporters after the game, "we're all one voice."

The NFL Players Association had a simple request from the team owners: Show us your books. The owners flat out refused, and the 2011 NFL football season was put on hold as a player lock out went into effect. "We are locked out," union president and former player Kevin Mawae wrote in a text message to the Associated Press. "We were informed today that players are no longer welcome at team facilities."[113] A lockout means there can be no communication between the players and their respective teams, while even health insurance is no longer paid to the players.

Although some readers may find it difficult to sympathize with the labor problems of professional football players, many of whom have multimillion-dollar contracts and bloated bonus packages, their lesson of solidarity should not be a wasted one. After all, if high-paid athletes understand the need to team together for their workplace rights, shouldn't nine-to-five working Americans feel the same? For the average worker, however, there is neither a prime-time television audience to hear our grievances, nor dedicated arbitrators fighting in our corner. While most professional athletes are in the financial position to endure one cancelled season, the average worker, who mostly survives paycheck to paycheck, is not. Indeed, once a particular job or entire industry has been made effectively redundant, the worker's season is over for what may be a very long and painful time-out.

With the rise of the lawless transnational corporations, an increasing number of Americans are becoming mere spectators to this winner-take-all economy. At the same time, workers are simply too afraid of risking their positions by demanding democratic representation in their myriad workplaces. Our business leaders are responsible for creating this palpable atmosphere of fear throughout the corporate jungle; corporations play on the

---

113 Howard Fendrich, "Lockout, Decertification Leave NFL in Limbo," Associated Press, March 3, 2011.

fear factor while enforcing the most egregious labor practices. As Francis Fukuyama pointed out, "An American chief executive exercises authoritarian powers of which a politician could only dream," and is held accountable in his actions only to a board of directors, which enables him to "hire, fire, make mergers or divest divisions at will."[114] Indeed, the captains of big business are able to act with total impunity, and this has created a veritable reign of fear throughout every sector of the economy. So the question, then, is how do we ensure that worker rights are respected in the face of these radical, oppressive conditions? Naturally, democracy is the answer.

"The mission of democratic statecraft…," wrote Arthur M. Schlesinger Jr. "is to give society a chance of controlling the energies let loose by science and technology. Democratic leadership is the art of fostering and managing innovation in the service of a free community."[115] Relying on labor unions in their present form to tame the best of the modern corporation is simply wishful thinking. Yet, the American people need some sort of democratic representation inside the walls of the corporate fortress or they will be oppressed at every opportunity. A person need not be a Marxist to understand a very simple universal truth: Without vibrant representation in the workplace, the individuals at the top of the corporate pyramid will exploit the people below them in the eternal quest for greater profit.

Corporate America is no longer bound by the old rules of the lumbering industrial era, when it was possible for workers to call a strike, halt production, and attract some sort of public attention to their cause. And there is no such thing as a workers' constitution to ensure life, liberty, and the pursuit of happiness for those toiling silently inside corporate fiefdoms across the land. This must change, or our experiment in globalization, not to mention the American Dream, will never be realized—at least not in a way that our Founding Fathers could possibly have imagined. As things now

---

114 Francis Fukuyama, "Trump Bid Reveals the Myth of the CEO President," *Financial Times*, April 28, 2011.
115 Arthur M. Schlesinger Jr., *The Cycles of American History* (Boston: Houghton Mifflin Company, 1986), 422.

stand, only the transnational corporations are in the position to achieve the American Dream. This must change. What the average American requires most today is democratic representation and fair conditions both in the workplace and in society at large. The following are some suggestions as to how that may be achieved.

DON'T EAT THE RICH, TAX THEM

The irony of our times is that corporations fought to achieve "personhood," yet do not want to do the two things required by every blood-and-flesh person: die and pay taxes.

It would be a safe bet to say that General Electric, the country's largest corporation, had a better 2010 than most Americans. Indeed, the granddaddy of US corporations posted profits of $14.2 billion, with $5.1 billion of that total deriving from domestic sales in the United States. Now, considering that the United States is trying to find some traction to extract itself from a deep recession, it would not hurt to have some of those corporate tax dollars recycling themselves back into the economy, maybe even assisting those citizens who were not as fortunate as GE was during the downturn. So what share of that $14 billion profit by GE went back to Uncle Sam? Not a single copper penny. That's right—nothing.

General Electric's "extraordinary success," tooted the *New York Times*, "is based on an aggressive strategy that mixes fierce lobbying for tax breaks and innovative accounting that enables it to concentrate its profits offshore." Such a strategy, the apologetic article continues, "have pushed down the corporate share of the nation's tax receipts from 30 percent of all federal revenue in the mid-1950s to 6.6 percent in 2009."[116]

Aside from sophisticated tax shelters that help corporations like GE to avoid their tax duty, the fact that so many US corporations have set up shop overseas also gives them privileges not available to regular people. Companies such as General Electric with

---

116   David Kosieniewski, "G.E.'s Strategies Let It Avoid Taxes Altogether," *New York Times*, March 24, 2011.

overseas operations do not have to pay US taxes if those profits are not brought back to American shores. So while these companies move work overseas, destroying potential jobs back home, they also hoard the mother lode of their earnings in foreign banks, while denying the US government its fair share of the tax harvest. General Electric, of course, painting itself as the victim of excessive government intrusion, says that its money-saving measures are necessary to compete with its rivals, as well as bring home the bacon for its demanding shareholders. "GE is committed to acting with integrity in relation to our tax obligations," said Anne Eisele, a company spokesperson, as quoted in the abovementioned *Times* article. "We are committed to complying with tax rules and paying all legally obliged taxes. At the same time, we have a responsibility to our shareholders to legally minimize our costs."

But the story gets better. Buried below the shocking news of GE's zero tax payments, it was duly reported that the company has been on something of a spending binge. "General Electric says it plans to buy a 90 percent stake in French electrical equipment developer Converteam in a deal GE values at $3.2 billion," the Associated Press reported. "The deal, which is expected to close during the third quarter, is the latest of $11 billion in acquisitions by GE. GE also has acquired Dresser Inc., Wellstream Holdings, Lineage Power Holdings and Well Support in the past six months."[117]

Clearly, General Electric, as well as hundreds of other wealthy US corporations, is not acting like a responsible citizen. In fact, the companies are acting utterly obscene in the name of pleasing their top executives and shareholders. By allowing corporations to masquerade as individual citizens, and empowered with all of the rights thereof, we have allowed a small franchise of individuals to severely distort the American Dream. The rallying call during the American War of Independence was "no taxation without representation." Today, in order to adapt to the radically changing times, we must demand, "No incorporation without taxation." But demanding that corporations and other wealthy Americans pay their fair tax share is not viewed as "common sense" to all.

---

117 "GE to Buy Converteam in $3.2B Deal," Associated Press, March 29, 2011.

Corporate America regularly complains about the 35 percent corporate tax rate, lobbying Congress for changes in the tax law, yet is able to exploit every tax loophole to its advantage. Corporations enjoy all the freedoms that come with being incorporated, while suffering none of the duties and demands. Those are duly passed off onto the law-abiding consumers.

Americans rightly believe that everybody should be rewarded for hard work and skills; at the same time, however, they reject the notion that nobody has dues to return to society. Yet many of the richest Americans have become so enchanted with their own success that they refuse to pay their fair share of the tax burden, hiring tax consultants with a special knack for manipulating every loophole in the tax code. Today, not only are corporate executives earning more than average Americans than ever before, corporations are paying the lowest tax rate in decades. According to the *Wall Street Journal*, quoting a report by the Congressional Budget Office, "[T]otal corporate federal taxes paid fell to 12.1% of profits earned from activities within the U.S. in fiscal 2011," which represents the lowest level "since at least 1972. And well below the 25.6% companies paid on average from 1987 to 2008."[118] Here is the really disturbing part of the story: "Companies paid just $181 billion in federal corporate taxes in fiscal 2011, about 8% of the $2.3 trillion in total revenue collected by the federal government. That's down from 15% of the total in 2007." For anybody who thinks that corporations are bearing too much of the tax load, consider this: "Individuals (you and me)… paid $1.1 trillion in income taxes last year." So all of those too-big-to-fail companies, veritable empires that are not limited by any national borders, pay a mere 10 percent of the tax load that the American people pay. Is it right that the poor and the middle class are always expected to pick up the tab for the rich after every feast?[119]

---

118 Damian Paletta, "With Tax Break, Corporate Tax Rate Is Lowest in Decades," *Wall Street Journal*, February 3, 2012.

119 Transnational corporations "shift the burden of paying for our national security and homeland security and other public services to small businesses and family taxpayers, who play by the rules and do engage in…shenanigans," said US Representative Lloyd Doggett,

Meanwhile, despite the fact that tax rates are already in the basement corporations continue to conceal their earnings from the tax man. According to a study commissioned by the Tax Justice Network, the "global super-rich elite had at least $21 trillion hidden in secret tax havens by the end of 2010."[120] According to the author of the study, James Henry, a former chief economist, the lost tax estimates "is large enough to make a significant difference to the finances of many countries." This stolen money, meanwhile, is "compensated" by painful austerity measures pushed onto the people.

Is it just coincidence that at the same time corporate tax rates are super low, corporate executive pay is also pushing against the salary ceiling? "The head of a typical public company made $9.6 million in 2011," according to the Associated Press. "That was up more than 6 percent from the previous year, and is the second year in a row of increases (the article reports that the average American worker would have to labor 244 years to make what the boss of a company earns in one)."[121] Equally disturbingly is the news agency's admission that the executive earnings rate is also the highest since "AP began tracking executive compensation in 2006." That is, two years before the Great Recession made landfall.

So how is corporate America spending this tax-free slush fund? According to a report by the nonpartisan advocacy group Public Campaign, thirty major US corporations spent more money lobbying Congress than they paid in federal income taxes between 2008 and 2010 (which comes out to about $400,000 every day). "Despite a growing federal deficit and the widespread economic instability that has swept the U.S. since 2008, the companies in question managed to accumulate profits of $164 billion between 2008 and 2010, while receiving combined tax rebates totalling almost $11 billion," the *International Business Times* reported. "Public Campaign reports these companies spent about $476 million during

---

as quoted by Jesse Drucker, "Tax 'Shenanigans' Turn U.S. Sales to Foreign Income with Billions Offshore," *Bloomberg*, July 23, 2010.

120 "Tax 'Hidden' by Global Super-Rich Worth $21tn," BBC News, July 22, 2012.

121 Christina Rexrode, "Profits at Big U.S. Companies Broke Records Last Year, and So Did Pay for CEOs," Associated Press, May 25, 2012.

the same period to lobby the U.S. Congress, as well as another $22 million on federal campaigns, while in some instances laying off employees and increasing executive compensation."[122]

Meanwhile, many on the political right continue whistling the old tune that keeping taxes low for the rich will somehow redound to the benefit of society as a whole. This is already been proved as a blatant lie. James K. Galbraith has demonstrated that the belief that tax cuts would stimulate economic growth was part of a sweeping experiment in supply-side Reaganomics that ultimately failed. "Supply-side tax cuts have no detectable effect on work effort, or savings, or investment," says Galbraith, who formerly served as executive director of the Joint Economic Committee of the US Congress. "Cuts in government spending are neither necessary nor sufficient for productivity gain. These are facts now well absorbed by practical policymakers, around whom the vestiges of past conservative verities hang in tatters."[123]

In fact, supply-side economics seems to be nothing more than an apologetic rationale to explain why the elite should feel no compulsion to contribute anything back to society, the very place where they made their riches in the first place. Increasingly, and especially in light of Barack Obama's failure to end the Bush-era tax cuts for the wealthy, the American people are beginning to sense that they are being isolated from the great American franchise. Indeed, the fabled "road to happiness" seems to exist only in fabled fenced-in communities far from the American heartland. We are beginning to see some tragic consequences as a result of this intolerable situation.

"On a day when the Internal Revenue Service came under literal attack [that is, the day that Joseph Stack, a failed entrepreneur, crashed his small plane into an IRS office in Austin, Texas], the agency reports that the nation's 44 highest-earning households reported an average income of $345 million in 2007—up 31% from 2006—and that their average tax bill fell to a 15-year

---

122 Ashley Portero, "30 Major U.S. Corporations Paid More to Lobby Congress than Income Taxes, 2008–2010," *International Business Times*, December 9, 2011.
123 Galbraith, *The Predator State*, 9.

low," *USA Today* reported.[124] It remains to be seen how many other American citizens, pushed to the edge of economic despair, will resort to irrational behavior.

As already acknowledged, there have always existed definite divisions between the rich and poor members of any given society. Nobody would deny this, or suggest that such a situation could realistically cease. It would be difficult, however, to cite another period in US history when the chasm between these eternally clashing groups has been so dangerous and dramatic. Not only is this extremely undesirable as far as national security goes, but it poses a great risk to the entire globalization project. While admitting to the folly of achieving full egalitarianism, the next reasonable thing to do is balance the tax scales to reflect income disparities, with the ultimate goal of lessening the chasm between rich and poor. It is important to note that it is just not the economic "have-nots" who are warning of a social cataclysm if the situation is not remedied.

One of the most outspoken advocates for increasing the taxes of the wealthy just happens to be the third-richest individual on the planet. Speaking before a gathering at Fortune's Most Powerful Women Summit, Warren Buffet – to the chagrin of his peers - was brave enough to admit that he paid the lowest tax rate of anyone in his office, including "secretaries who answer the phone and the cleaning lady," before advocating a major overhaul of the US tax system. In a recent editorial, Buffett argued for a minimum tax for the wealthy. "I would suggest 30 percent of taxable income between $1 million and $10 million, and 35 percent on amounts above that," Buffett wrote. "A plain and simple rule like that will block the efforts of lobbyists, lawyers and contribution-hungry legislators to keep the ultrarich paying rates well below those incurred by people with income just a tiny fraction of ours."[125] Only a "minimum tax on very high incomes" will protect the nation from "warriors for the wealthy," he stressed.

---

124 "IRS: 400 Richest Averaged $345M in '07 Income, 16% Tax Rate," *USA Today*, February 18, 2010.
125 Warren Buffett, "A Minimum Tax for the Wealthy," *New York Times*, November 25, 2012.

Yet such prudent advice is regularly ignored by US senators who demanded—at a time when the government needs to raise its $14.3 trillion "debt ceiling"—a two-year extension on Bush-era tax cuts for families earning more than $250,000 annually. They even got an indefinite extension on their tax-free inheritances. Such behavior only fortifies the belief that the corporate rich and superrich, despite their obscene salaries and bonuses, not to mention bailouts, believe they owe nothing back to the system that gave them their wealth in the first place.

No man is an island, and every wealthy individual has debts to return to society. Instead, many of these narcissistic individuals, spoiled by the new-age religion of hyper individualism, cannot think past the front door of their forty-five-room mansions. "I achieved all of this myself, so why should I give a dime to anybody?" they ask. Such an attitude shows how far we as a nation have wandered from the basic tenets that once upon a time made America great. Many of our most successful individuals today believe the best interest is self-interest. In some cases, this is correct. Yet they cynically believe that every individual who has failed to "make it" is either a welfare queen or simply lazy and undeserving. This too is sometimes correct. However, the vast majority of people falling through the gaping cracks today do not fit into such narrow, politically manipulated categories. The people struggling to make ends meet today are hardworking individuals, attempting to raise families while decent jobs are being shipped overseas. When these people read stories about how the other half is living, while failing to pay their fair share of taxes, this only turns our melting pot into a pressure cooker that promises to explode at some point.

It would be wise to recall that even the cutthroat Romans had a sense of *noblesse oblige,* a term that dates back to ancient times when the nobles actually went into battle to defend the interests of the common people. Our European ancestors understood the importance of defending the interests of those at the bottom of the social ladder. Indeed, the risks associated with defending the interests of the less privileged members of society are far less than the risks of not doing anything at all. Compare the Romans' sense of duty with our hyper individualism and culture of greed. Apart from public acts of charity and philanthropy (which have a curious way of coming across as egoistic and self-serving, not to mention humiliating and demeaning for those on the receiving end), there are no built-in methods for lifting the marginalized members of society out of their material, spiritual, and intellectual poverty.[126] "Indeed, you can usually tell when the concepts of democracy and citizenship are weakening," John Ralston Saul, an author and essayist, once said. "There is an increase in the role of charity and in the worship of volunteerism. These represent the elite citizen's imitation of noblesse oblige; that is, of pretending to be aristocrats and oligarchs, as opposed to being citizens." Meanwhile, "social climbing" and "income mobility" is becoming an increasingly slippery affair for an increasing percentage of the population.

The lack of social mobility inside the corporate fortress is increasingly linked to undue privilege within the system. This is becoming more of a political question based on power and influence, as opposed to an economic question based on common sense, fairness, and rationality. "When it comes to defending the interests of the rich," writes the economist Paul Krugman, "the normal rules of civilized (and rational) discourse no longer apply."[127] Krugman goes on to explain what differentiates the rich from the rest of the population. "It's partly a matter of campaign contributions, but it's also a matter of social pressure, since politicians spend a lot of time hanging out with the wealthy. So when the rich feel the prospect of paying an extra 3 or 4 percent of their income in taxes, politicians feel their pain—feel it much more acutely, it's clear, than they feel the pain of families who are losing their jobs, their houses, and their hopes."

The wealthy corporate class, in order to maintain excessive lifestyles, is denying a significant number of individuals the right to receive an adequate education, exposure to high culture (or

---

126 Oscar Wilde, in his play *The Ideal Husband*, commenting on public acts of charity: "Philanthropy seems…to have become the refuge of people who wish to annoy their fellow-creatures." O. Henry put into the mouth of one of his hungry characters in the short story *The Cop and the Anthem*, "If not in coin—you must pay in humiliation of spirit for every benefit received at the hands of philanthropy."
127 Paul Krugman, "The Angry Rich," *New York Times*, September 19, 2010.

at least a respectable culture), and reasonable opportunities for economic independence. The corporate elite would rather hoard the mother lode of corporate profits for themselves in the belief, which has been disproven by the recent crisis, that they know better how to spend the extra money. This greed and avarice is working to thwart the overall development of American society, while embittering millions of people who no longer see any justice or fairness in the system. Most disturbing, they see no hope of escaping their inherited condition of poverty.

"Nowadays in America," *Financial Times* reported, "you have a smaller chance of swapping your lower-income bracket for a higher one than in almost any other developed economy." [128] The grim conclusion: "To invert the classic Horatio Alger stories, in today's America if you are born in rags, you are likelier to stay in rags than in almost any corner of old Europe." This a startling turn of events for a nation that has for years served as a beacon of opportunity in a sea of iniquity for the world's "huddled masses yearning to breathe free," to quote part of the poem inscribed on the base of the Statue of Liberty.

A fair system of taxation, which works to the advantage of average income earners, as opposed to those who can afford to find tax shelters, is essential in an age of supercorporations, which hoard the lion's share of the wealth at the expense of those who deserve and need it the most. The current situation regarding corporate tax rates goes far in explaining exactly how the "elite" came to manipulate our political process. Clearly, not every saved tax dollar is being recycled back into the economy in order to spur research and development of new products and, by extension, job growth. In fact, judging by the torrent of donations being made to lobbying and special interest groups, many of those dollars are being used to buy a particular political agenda. Think about that. The dollars that we as consumers spend to buy the dizzying array of products from corporations are being turned around and used to fund a political agenda that in all likelihood is detrimental to ourselves and our families. Moreover, more than one economist has

---

128   Edward Luce, "Goodbye, American Dream," *Financial Times*, August 1, 2010.

argued that lowering the tax burden on the wealthiest Americans does nothing to stimulate economic growth. "What do workers, or anyone else, get out of the process of accumulation?" asked James K. Galbraith, former executive director of the Joint Economic Committee of the US Congress. "*Nothing.* The acts of saving and investment are purely private. The benefits are therefore purely private. Any benefit accruing to anyone other than the original saver or capitalist would have to be counted an inefficiency."[129]

There is one final way of making sure that America remains an egalitarian nation, which is committed to protecting the least fortunate: Tax the very individuals who steered the global economy into the rocks. According to Dean Baker, from Scholar Strategy Network, US hedge fund managers "borrow large amounts of other people's money and use it to make heavily leveraged bets in money markets."[130] Following the Great Recession of 2008, all of us are familiar with what happens when such speculation goes wrong: The global economy suffers severe economic turbulence, while it is the average taxpayer who is left holding the bill.

According to Baker, these "speculative maneuvers yield enormous windfalls to a few winners," while providing "little or no benefit to the American economy." Furthermore, the largely unregulated gambling house of the American financial sector "is now a drain on the real economy and is one of the main contributors to rapidly expanding inequalities of wealth and income." So how can we get rid of this "financial bloat?" Baker advises "a very small tax on financial transactions," which would "raise the cost of rapid-fire speculation...and help reduce the federal budget deficit." For those who have a tendency to scream in pain whenever they hear the word "tax," Baker has some sober news: It won't hurt because financial trading costs "have been falling rapidly over the last three decades as a result of the advance of computer technology. The 0.03 percent tax rate...would merely raise trading costs back to where they were 5-10 years ago."

---

129 James K. Galbraith, *The Predator State* (New York: Free Press, 2008), 29. Italics in the original.
130 Dean Baker, "What a Tax on Wall Street Speculation Can Do for America," Scholars Strategy Network, July 2012.

Now all we have to do is prevent the corporate lobbyists in Washington from scaring our politicians from doing the right thing.

GUESS WHAT, US WORKERS? YOU'RE RICH!

One of corporate America's most guarded secrets involves not only the value of employee pension funds, but how this massive stash of private cash is being mishandled. According to the most conservative estimates, pension funds are worth $20 trillion in assets, the largest amount for any category of investment, bigger than mutual funds, currency reserves, sovereign wealth funds, private equity, and even the notorious hedge funds. And it is largely through this immense treasure trove that US companies, borrowing from this available equity, are able to keep their R&D departments running smoothly. Yet following the financial fiasco of 2007, hundreds of billions of dollars of these funds went down the drain, practically unreported, leaving many retiree hopefuls in dire straits. That is because many US companies invested much of their employee retirement funds into high-risk portfolios. Today many retirement-age employees are waking up to the reality that the money they were promised is simply not there.

Much like subprime mortgages, which contained enough perplexing small print to sink the ship of the global economy, pension funds also contain their share of cryptic conditions that promise to derail more than one retirement dream. Despite the risks involved, many companies unwisely dumped their employee pensions into the tainted mortgage market. As the *Economist* summed up the situation for millions of unsuspecting Americans: "The collapse of mighty banks like Lehman Brothers and Bear Stearns are bad news for anyone with a pension fund."[131]

---

131 "Endless Culture War," *Economist*, A Special Briefing, page 23, October 4, 2008. According to a report by the Urban Institute, a Washington-based independent research group, about $2.7 trillion was lost in 401(k) and individual retirement accounts between 2007 and 2009. See Troy McCullen, *ABC News*, October 15, 2009.

The *Financial Times* was yet another foreign news outlet that picked up the slippery ball that the US mainstream media fumbled: "As the US stock market sold off 37 percent during 2008, investors in target date funds ['target date funds' are yet another sophisticated investment tool used to invest in pensions, and much of it went into the blind speculation of subprime mortgages] of vintage year 2010 expected to retire in a couple of years with their capital more or less intact," the British business paper reported, before quoting Mary Shapiro, head of the Securities and Exchange Commission, who broke the news as unobtrusively as possible that much of the money evaporated into thin air during the crisis: "The reality of [the pensions] was quite surprising to many investors last year," Shapiro told a public hearing of the SEC on June 25, 2009.[132] She added in her testimony the following shocker: "The average loss in 2008 among 31 funds with a 2010 target date was almost 25 percent, but perhaps even more surprising were their widely varying performance results—returns of 2010 target date funds during 2008 range from minus 3.6 percent to minus 41 percent."

The article went on to provide a rather astounding comment by Mark Warshawsky, director of retirement research with consultant Towers Watson. "A lot of the concern about 2008's returns relates to investors' confusion over what target dates are," he said. "Some investors have expected guarantees on assets or income when they retired." But isn't that the whole idea of investing into a pension plan: To guarantee that a person can comfortably retire from his or her place of employment after many years of dedicated service? Now millions of personal pension plans, thanks to a lot of tampering by corporate America, are at grave risk of not being paid.

Perhaps the individuals who sold these "sophisticated" investment schemes somehow believed that American workers would be willing to gamble with their retirement packages. That argument seems highly suspect, especially since most Americans count down the days to their retirement. Furthermore, how many American workers even know that their pensions are at serious risk? Millions

---

132 John Keefe, "Fixing a Failed US Pension Scheme," *Financial Times* (FTfm), January 25, 2009.

of American workers, by entrusting their employers to manage their pension funds, got burned in the latest meltdown and will not be able to ride off into the sunset according to their original plans. Yet there has been no bailout plan to rescue these lost funds as there were with the banks and corporations. Many pensions are simply gone with the wind. Thus, it would make sense that if corporate America is gambling with our pension accounts, possibly ruining our retirement dreams in the process, we should have some say as to how these funds get invested. If nothing else, there needs to be much greater transparency in worker retirement funds.

A report by the Organization for Economic Cooperation and Development (OECD)[133] highlights the danger, in the worlds of the OECD itself, "of the financial, economic and fiscal crisis turning into a *social* crisis (italics in the original)," because both public and private pension schemes have been "affected negatively by the crisis." In the United States, pension funds shed more than a quarter of their value during the downturn, and the reason is directly connected with the irresponsible and risky way our money was invested.

The countries that suffered the worst losses to their pension schemes, Ireland, Australia, and the United States (-37.5, -26.7, and -26.2 percent, respectively), differed dramatically from other nations, such as Mexico, Czech Republic, and Germany (-5.2, -7.2, and -8.5, respectively), in terms of the percentage of money lost in their pension funds for one simple reason: "Stocks made up the majority of pension funds' portfolios in English-speaking countries before the crisis hit," the OECD briefing paper explains. In contrast, investment in stocks from pension funds made up "around 10% of portfolios in the Czech and Slovak Republics, and Mexico." This is yet another example where government responsibility—ensuring that its people are able to retire safely and without any strings attached—has taken a backseat to corporate malfeasance and recklessness. The situation takes on an entirely differ-

---

133 "Pensions and the Crisis," Organization for Economic Cooperation and Development briefing that sets out the key findings on pensions and the crisis from OECD *Pensions at a Glance 2009.*

ent shade when it is realized that, according to the OECD, private financial resources make up 45 percent of retirement incomes in the United States.

Considering the risk involved in even retiring comfortably, this is just one area where American citizens can reclaim some of their democratic rights inside the corporate universe. Employees must have far greater supervisory powers over this vast amount of money and the way it gets invested. After all, we earned it! For starters, a portion of the invested pension fund money—assuming that it is invested in a responsible, low-risk way and actually turns a profit—could support a nationwide worker-training program. This would be an investment few could argue against, since most jobs these days have become temporary luxuries; people must receive constant retraining and education to stay competitive in the job markets. Another alternative is to provide an unemployment fund for workers who lose their jobs and need to cover the rent payment. Still another is a union-backed credit union that provides low-interest loans to employees. The possibilities are endless. Yet to date US corporations continue to invest their employee pensions the way they believe is most advantageous—for them.

The lack of supervision over the workers' retirement fund, which corporations play with at will, perfectly proves the central thesis: The voracious greed of the corporate world needs a healthy dose of democracy. History has repeatedly proved mankind's predilection for evil, greed, and outright violence when the firewalls against immoral behavior have been weakened or removed. As it stands, democracy and a sense of social responsibility is glaringly absent from where it should be most prevalent in a capitalist-based democracy—in the heart of the business world. The American people need democracy to exist inside the corporate universe before we can consider it safe to endorse capitalism inside a democracy. At the same time, corporate power must be removed from the halls of political power. Otherwise, the country is heading for nothing less than tyranny.

CHAPTER IV
Reclaiming the
Commons from Corporate Power

"The classical economic idea that another's gain is at the expense of one's own loss is replaced by the idea that enhancing the well-being of others amplifies one's own well-being."

— JEREMY RIFKIN, *"THE EMPHATIC CIVILIZATION"*

Most Americans, despite the destructive dynamics of globalization, are still intimately familiar with the idea of Main Street, those bustling zones of activity where citizens gather for economic, social, and political pursuits. Taken as a whole, these avenues create the colorful quilt of national life. The idea of Main Street, however, is not a singularly American phenomenon, nor is it modern per se. Venues set aside for social interaction have been an integral part of the human story since the Greeks gathered at the agora and the Romans at their famed Forum many centuries ago. As the ancients inherently understood, the smooth functioning of Main Street and its many diverse enterprises was critical for the health and well-being of the nation at large. These meeting places generate the social electricity needed for uniting the country at large. Therefore, given the link between a vibrant community and the overall health of the people, we cannot afford to be indifferent to what is happening inside America.

Today, Americans across the country are reporting a sense of breakdown in their communities, a sense of aimless drift and the feeling that something has been severed from the heart of our diverse living spaces. Or perhaps what is missing is the heart itself. Due to the invasion of corporate power, modest, independently owned business establishments—coffee shops, grocery stores, clothes stores, restaurants, hardware stores, and pharmacies, to name just a few—that once gave the town center its dynamic character and pulse are now on the verge of extinction. In some twisted interpretation of an Ayn Rand novel, corporations believe it is their right to crush the small-town business proprietor, not to mention the town itself.

Town and country are being forced to accommodate econo-mies of unnatural size, as the inhabitants must learn to adapt to an influx of sprawling megamalls, hyperstores, and supermarkets. While these venues provide consumers with an intensely private shopping experience, they give precious little in terms of social cohesiveness that comes from an active, interconnected citizen-ship. In the shift from local to global, what we gain in terms of material choice is nullified by what we are losing in the spiritual sense of community.

"Because of corporate consolidation, businesses are no longer owned locally and Main Street is gone," notes the journalist and author William Kleinknecht. "Companies made over many times by mergers and forced to tailor every decision to stock market prices have little loyalty to communities or people. Commerce becomes alien, unreliable, globalized. Plants are closed and com-panies are downsized, families uprooted, communities left without anchors."[134] Kleinknecht goes on to describe the oppressive atmos-phere that has settled on many communities and neighborhoods with the arrival of the corporate giants. "There is an eerie silence

---

134 William Kleinknecht, *The Man Who Sold the World* (New York: Nation Books, 2009), xii.

even in the center of town," he writes, "a listlessness that reminds a visitor that the time in this country when such communities had relevance and vitality is coming to a close....Everything that is inspiring or pleasing to the eye belongs to the past."[135]

The inhabitants of our local environs are considered valuable only in direct proportion to their ability to shop and spend, as opposed to participating in the political arena. Long before former President George W. Bush, in the aftermath of the terror attacks of 9/11, beseeched Americans to "perform their patriotic duty" by shopping, we as a nation have come to believe that mindless consumerism qualifies as social and civic participation. Of course, it does not. Even the term *citizen* has been largely deleted from the national vernacular and substituted with the narrow and demeaning stamp *consumer*. Those in the former group lend their expertise to the community; the latter can do nothing more than grab what is available. By selling out our political voice for ephemeral, hedonistic pursuits, we have committed irreparable damage to our fragile democratic franchise, squandering the vital electricity of human relations that must flow unobstructed through our communities.

At the same time, we have become accomplices to the destruction of the irreplaceable "mom and pop" franchises, which do much more than simply provide would-be entrepreneurs with an income. Individual proprietorship provides citizens with a vital sense of autonomy and independence, which has been an integral part of the American experience, better known as the American Dream, since our nation's founding. It is also responsible for building the foundation of cooperation and trust necessary for the success of any community.

In her landmark book on urban planning, *The Death and Life of Great American Cities*, Jane Jacobs documented the "extra-merchandising services" that small neighborhood entrepreneurs provide to the local community almost as unconscious gestures, which gives urban living spaces a sense of much-needed "balance." Here, Jacobs provides a description of the "extra-merchandising

---

135   Ibid, 20.

services" provided by the proprietors of a neighborhood candy store: *"One ordinary morning last winter…Bernie, and his wife, Ann, supervised the small children crossing at the corner on the way to P.S. 41, as Bernie always does because he sees the need; lent an umbrella to one customer and a dollar to another; took custody of two keys; took in some packages for people in the next building who were away; lectured two youngsters who asked for cigarettes; gave street directions; took custody of a watch to give the repairman across the street when he opened later; gave out information on the range of rents in the neighborhood to an apartment seeker; listened to a tale of domestic difficulty and offered reassurance; etc., etc. "*[136]

With such intense personal interaction with the local population, proprietors enjoyed a high social standing and improved self-esteem. "Storekeepers…enjoy an excellent social status," Jacobs continues. "Their advice, as men and women of common sense and experience, is sought and respected. They are well known as individuals, rather than unknown as class symbols." It is exactly this sort of atmosphere that the corporate hyperstores render impossible to deliver due to their sheer size and dislocation from the nerve center of the town, which in many cases exists only in name. "The general store proprietor," as described in *American Business History,* "was a citizen of eminent importance. His store was the center of village life. It was the gathering place for news and gossip. His advice was sought in both business and domestic matters, and his influence was felt in almost all areas of town and village life."[137]

The physical and spiritual construction of Main Street, USA is a lengthy process that requires years of hard work and dedication to complete. Yet, in one afternoon, a single corporation can call a meeting with local officials, flash wads of cash, and destroy the work of many generations. Corporations, guided by the single-minded goal of maximizing their profits, are attempting to unite the concept of community together under one massive roof. Such a narrow, destructive strategy serves only to accommodate

---

136   Jane Jacobs, *The Death and Life of Great American Cities* (New York: Random House, 1961), 61.

137   Herman E. Kroos, *American Business History* (Englewood Cliffs, New Jersey: Prentice Hall, 1972), 189.

their wealthy shareholders, who invariably live far away from the destruction zone. These corporate predators have no respect for the dignity and pride of the communities they enter. They wish only to feed off the host until all the life is drained, and then they move on in search of their next prey.

Meanwhile, the presence of these corporate boxes far removed from the heart of the local society does much more than disfigure the aesthetic face of our communities. It has been proved to cause men and women to experience "alienation" inside their own country; strangers in their own home. The historian William Appleman Williams expressed this idea by arguing that for entrepreneurs "the loss of meaningful participation in the productive economic system would lead wage earners to feel alienated from the political system."[138] Just as a feeling of alienation affects the worker in relation to his job, it also applies to the alienation that citizens feel in their own society.

Around the time of the Second World War, Dr. Erich Fromm had already predicted the rise of the corporate forces that would go on to conquer not only our neighborhoods but the nation at large. Because it perfectly describes our present situation, it is worth reprinting his comment in its entirety: "The concentration of capital (not of wealth) in certain sectors of our economic system restricts the possibilities for the success of individual initiative, courage, and intelligence. In those sectors in which monopolistic capital has won its victories the economic independence of many has been destroyed. For those who struggle on, especially for a large part of the middle class, the fight assumes the character of a battle against such odds that the feeling of confidence in personal initiative and courage is replaced by a feeling of powerlessness and hopelessness. An enormous though secret power over the whole of society is exercised by a small group, on the decisions of which depend the fate of a large part of society....The small or middle-sized businessman who is virtually threatened by the overwhelming power of superior capital may very well continue to make profits

---

138 David Noble, *The End of History* (Minneapolis: University of Minnesota Press, 1985), 123.

and to preserve his independence; but the threat hanging over his head has increased his insecurity and powerlessness far beyond what it used to be. In his fight against monopolistic competitors he is staked against giants, whereas he used to fight against equals."[139]

As this comment proves, sociologists and researchers from earlier generations were acutely perceptive to the rise of corporate power simply because it was a radical new phenomenon— a phenomenon that the majority of the erudite minority vehemently condemned. The most optimistic observers believed that the people would eventually regain—the argument put tremendous faith in the natural morality of man—democratic control over the runaway corporations, or that the state would intervene and regulate their activity for the benefit of the people and society as a whole (this was the essence of debate in the presidential campaign between Woodrow Wilson and Theodore Roosevelt in 1912). As Benjamin Barber explained the irrational optimism, "In America, the confidence in the omnipotence of markets has been transformed into a foreign policy that assumes internationalizing markets is tantamount to democratizing them and that human freedom is secured the minute nations or tribes sign on to the dogmas of free trade."[140]

Although every business venture big or small must take into account the bottom line in order to remain solvent, corporate America has taken this consideration to such an extreme that its continued existence can no longer be justified. Our fragile neighborhoods have turned into battlefields for transnational corporations to fight over, instead of flourishing, wholesome places for raising families and achieving our personal dreams. The hostile corporate takeover of town and country has deprived men and women of their long-cherished rugged individualism, which we have shown is the very essence and defining trait of the American citizen.[141] The results of this usurpation are devastatingly clear. The residents of our local communities have been severely

---

139 Erich Fromm, *Escape From Freedom* (New York, 1941), 192, italics added.
140 Barber, 239.
141 The Institute for Policy Studies concluded in a recent study that of the world's largest economies, fifty-one are now corporations while forty-nine are countries. Liberalization

separated from each other in the economic, social, and political realms, and this change signals the death of the community at large. The unprecedented rise in violence and violent behavior is another symptom that Main Street, USA, has taken a turn for the worse. The radical new arrangement of our living spaces hinders the chances for civic awareness, democracy, and even simple trust; as we have already demonstrated, there is a heavy democratic price to pay for allowing big business to run rampant through our communities. Meanwhile, one company, America's biggest employer, has become the poster child for corporate destructiveness run rampant.

WELCOME TO WAL-MART

Sam Walton, the founder of Wal-Mart, opened the doors to his first store in 1962 in Rogers, Arkansas. By following a very determined business strategy, five years later Wal-Mart had snowballed into eighteen stores, with almost $10 million in annual profit. Today, with over 1.2 million workers in the United States and total annual revenues of about $400 billion, Wal-Mart is much more than the sum of its parts. But can this corporation really be considered an American success story? From the perspective of the corporate boardroom and shareholder meetings, the answer is clear: Wal-Mart has made an infinitesimal percentage of the population very wealthy. Yet for an increasing number of hardworking Americans across the land, Wal-Mart has been nothing less than a social, economic, and political nightmare. In the words of one commentator, "Wal-Mart is there to destroy the competition and make a buck, not to build community or add to one that already exists."[142] Now, thousands of Americans, after witnessing the effects that Wal-Mart has had on other communities, are taking a

---

schemes have provided corporations "increasing levels of economic and political clout that are out of balance with tangible benefits they provide society."

The overall economic capacities of the top two hundred corporations are greater than all but the ten largest countries.

142   Bill Quinn, *How Wal-Mart is Destroying America* (Berkeley: Ten Speed Press, 1998), 20.

courageous stand to prevent this vampire retailer from entering their own neighborhoods. Needless to say, however, many of these unreported battles have been lost, while it seems that Wal-Mart has already won the war.

"Wal-Mart is not just the world's largest retailer," writes Charles Fishman. "It's the world's largest company—bigger than Exxon-Mobil, General Motors, and General Electric." If the monumental scale and scope of this single corporate venture is difficult to fathom, Fishman provides some basic comparisons. "Wal-Mart no longer has any rivals. It does more business than Target, Sears, Kmart, J.C. Penney, Safeway, and Kroger combined…It is, in fact, so big and so furtively powerful as to have become an entirely different order of corporate being."[143]

Despite, or because of its massive economic footprint, Wal-Mart is a huge recipient of US government assistance. According to a report by *The Nation*: "Wal-Mart is one of the biggest recipients of government subsidies, receiving tax breaks, free land, cash grants and other forms of public assistance, in addition to paying some of its workers so little that they also turn to the federal government for programs like the Supplemental Nutrition Assistance Program (SNAP)."[144] Yet America's biggest employer regularly falls back on the "jobs and consumer savings" argument to justify its deplorable behavior.

Considering the present economic downturn, it is admittedly difficult to argue against jobs and consumer savings, which is Wal-Mart's main argument for bringing the bulldozers into communities across the nation. But is this gargantuan corporation giving us the full story? Judging by everything that is at stake, we must take Wal-Mart to task, and seriously consider if this so-called "American success story" has translated into a healthier living environment for the millions of people who now live in the vicinity of one of Wal-Mart's thousands of stores nationwide.

One of Wal-Mart's favorite talking points for building yet another bloodless box beyond the town center is that it will pro-

---

143 Charles Fishman, "The Wal-Mart You Don't Know," FastCompany.com, December 1, 2003.
144 Allison Kilkenny, "Occupy Wal-Mart: Workers Plan Black Friday Protests," *The Nation*, November 20, 2012.

mote job creation in the targeted region. This argument has already been exposed as a blatant lie. When a Wal-Mart or Sam's Club enters a community, it naturally forces many smaller neighborhood stores out of business. Indeed, Wal-Mart has singlehandedly turned hundreds of once-bustling urban centers into veritable ghost towns. In other words, Wal-Mart provides "job opportunities" for the very same individuals who lost their jobs thanks to the arrival of Wal-Mart in the first place.

In an eye-opening academic study[145] tracing the effects of Wal-Mart on US employment levels, researchers were shocked to discover that not only did the opening of Wal-Mart stores not boost employment rates, but it actually lowered them. The study examines data from 1961, the year before the first Wal-Mart store opened, through 2004. In that period, the report showed, "Retail employment in the United States grew from 5.56 million to 15.06 million, or 271 percent, considerably faster growth than that of overall employment (242 percent)." The researchers calculated: "If each of the 3,066 stores present in January of 2005 reduced retail employment by our estimate of 147 workers relative to the counterfactual, then our estimates imply that, in the absence of Wal-Mart, retail employment would have instead grown to 15.51 million as of 2004, or 3 percent higher than the observed figure." The study's stunning conclusion: "Wal-Mart has negative rather than positive effects on net job creation in the retail sector."

To put the figures another way, the researchers conclude: "The employment results indicate that a Wal-Mart store opening reduces county-level retail employment by about 150 workers, implying that each Wal-Mart worker replaces approximately 1.4 retail workers. This represents a 2.7 percent reduction in the average retail employment. The payroll results indicate that Wal-Mart store openings lead to declines in county-level retail earnings of about $1.2 million, or 1.3 percent."

Wal-Mart also likes to boast that it is helping to invigorate America's lagging industrial base. The data tell a different story.

---

145 David Neumark, Junfu Zhang, and Stephen Ciccarella, "The Effects of Wal-Mart on Local Labor Markets," Institute for the Study of Labor, January 2007.

According to Walmartwatch.com, a website devoted to reporting the truth about this runaway company, Wal-Mart has dramatically increased the quantity of imported products sold in its stores. "In 2006, Wal-Mart imported $27 billion of Chinese goods. Wal-Mart's imports are responsible for 11% of the growth of the total U.S. trade deficit with China between 2001 and 2006."[146] Obviously, Wal-Mart is more interested in inflating its bottom line than it is in giving Americans some good factory jobs.

These statistics should serve as a wake-up call to millions of Americans who passively accept Wal-Mart's bogus claims that it is a boon to the national economy. Clearly, this is not the case. Not only is Wal-Mart hurting the national economy, it is also dragging down the wages of retail workers. The report pointed to the "highly-paid grocery workers," many of whom belong to the United Food and Commercial Workers (UFCW), "who may be harmed from competition with Supercenters."[147] This should come as no surprise, since it is well-known that Wal-Mart vigorously works behind the scenes to prevent its workers from forming any sort of labor union.

Some critics will respond that any criticism of the new global dynamics that are reshaping America is backward thinking. Those who cling to traditions are being overly nostalgic about a mythical "golden age" that was actually more tarnished than sparkling. Maybe the so-called "good old days," when privately owned shops dotted tree-lined boulevards, and each individual was somehow actively involved in the dynamics of his community, never really existed except in the vivid imaginations of our parents and grandparents. After all, we are all guilty of reflecting on the halcyon days of youth with a sense of awe and bewilderment; the "glorious past" has an uncanny way of reflecting back to the present through the imperfect lens of our subjectivity. So in order to discover at least part of the truth, let's turn back the hands of time with some help from the world of art.

---

146 "Supplier Relationships," The Center for Community & Corporate Ethics, August 1, 2008, http://walmartwatch.com/issues/supplier_relationships/.
147 Ibid, 35.

A REQUIEM FOR ROCKWELL'S AMERICA

Norman Rockwell (1894–1978), the American illustrator, spent the better part of his prolific career attempting to capture the spirit of small-town America through the medium of oil paint. Some of his most memorable paintings, published on the cover of the *Saturday Evening Post* over four decades (321 works in all), portray sentimental scenes of ordinary citizens going about their daily business in the public realm. In every Rockwell painting, a sense of civic duty, individual strength, and spiritual morality leaps out from the canvas. The more corrosive elements that now work to degrade American communities—crime, drugs, and pervasive violence, to name just a few—are total strangers in Rockwell's romantic America.

In one illustration, entitled *Shuffleton's Barbershop* (1950), Rockwell depicts members of a barbershop quartet rehearsing in the back room of the establishment. This painting, as is the case with most of Rockwell's work, conveys a much deeper message than is immediately perceived. With the empty shop appearing in the foreground, draped in shadows, the viewer's eye is drawn to the bright lights in the back of the shop where we can see the quartet is rehearsing. Here, Rockwell is conveying the message that it is the members of the community, as opposed to the business establishment itself, who are (or should be) the vital players on the local scene. The business, much like the theater, serves as a stage for bringing together a wide range of individual personalities in the great act of life. And it is inside these many diverse venues that important issues may be discussed and debated. Or the group may simply enjoy a good conversation, a pastime that is quickly becoming a lost art form in our virtual world of electronic-powered "social media." The main point is that in Rockwell's world, mindless consumerism is not the primary activity of the civic-minded citizen.

In another painting, *Cobbler Studying Doll's Shoe* (1921), Rockwell depicts the virtually extinct neighborhood cobbler taking the time—without pay, we may safely assume—to mend a doll for a little girl. The scene is so innocent and full of tenderness that we

101

are tempted to believe that the cobbler knows the name of the girl, her parents, and probably all of her relatives. Meanwhile, the cobbler, like the majority of the other local merchants and craftsmen from Rockwell's "idyllic" era, is a trusted member of his society who lends his personal assistance whenever possible. Although it is obvious that the cobbler is not performing his little act of "charity" with the hope of receiving recompense, the craftsman may rest assured that his unconscious act of generosity will be repaid in his own hour of need. These types of informal relationships, although seemingly trivial and unremarkable, act as the unbreakable thread that weaves its way gracefully and seamlessly through every viable community. Without these types of tight bonds among the people, there is little hope for sustaining a liveable community. Trust is the foundation stone upon which all livable neighborhoods are built.

Rockwell, through his realistic renderings, showed that the most important element of any business venture is not the business itself, but rather the individual personalities—both owners and customers—that breath life into it. Business, in order for it to be a truly successful venture, must act as a unifying catalyst, a boon for the neighborhood and neighbors, as opposed to a disruptive force as so many corporate ventures, artificially dropped into our neighborhoods like foreign fauna, have become. Today, with the ongoing demise of the quaint mom and pops, large, fast, and impersonal are becoming the keywords of these distracted, hyperactive times. This radical makeover of Main Street has led to a palpable atmosphere of fear inside the smallest towns. It has become a telling cliché that men can no longer sleep sound in the knowledge that they did not lock the front door of their homes.

Yet another problem with behemoth corporate ventures dropped haphazardly into our sensitive local areas is their dislocation and isolation from the city center. We are constructing our living spaces in a way that only serves to boost corporate profits. Indeed, in many cases, these new ventures have become a poor substitute for the city center themselves. It is practically impossible to visit these places without the use of an automobile. In fact, in many communities it appears almost strange and somehow suspicious to witness people walking. For many suburbanites, most errands big or small require two tons of motorized steel and glass. If our communities had been designed and constructed according to the needs of people—as opposed to the corporations—a simple trip to the grocery store and other daily errands could be easily accomplished on foot. This would allow us to actually get out of our cars and mingle face-to-face with our fellow citizens on the sidewalks of our tree-lined communities, as opposed to suffering attacks of road rage behind a plate-glass windshield.

By contrast, in each of Rockwell's "romantic" illustrations America's town and country possesses a recognizable human face where today's ubiquitous corporation is not yet dominating the scene; more important, it is a face that represents the small-town entrepreneur (as opposed to the anonymous "person" of the corporation) working side by side with other like-minded members of the community. Rockwell's numerous works are historically accurate portrayals of typical Americans congregating along Main Street, USA, in a heroic chapter of American history when commerce and trade did not completely overshadow the endeavors of personal men and women, that is, when it was still possible—and certainly desirable—to organize one's life as a rugged individual. In other words, Rockwell shows us "the details of life that are often overlooked."[148]

Today, in an effort by the world of art to capture the spirit of these corporate days of extreme materialism, realism has given way to cynicism as artists have no choice but to cast a weary, contemptible eye on the grim social realities that confront them. The 1960s pop artist Andy Warhol (1928–1987), for example, got his "fifteen minutes of fame" for his silk-screen prints that depicted mass-produced images of popular products, such as Heinz Baked Beans and Coca-Cola, as well as living, breathing commodities personified by the likes of Marilyn Monroe, Elizabeth Taylor, and Elvis Presley. Warhol's subject material and presentation, which overlapped the Rockwell years, signaled a radical break for the world of art, as well as the social realities of Main Street, USA.

---

148 Maureen Hart Hennessey and Anne Knutson, *Norman Rockwell, Pictures for the American People* (Henry Luce Foundation, 1999), 64.

Warhol, who hailed from the former industrial city of Pittsburgh, sought to portray the new realities of our mass-production culture, even mass-producing the very "star quality" of celebrities in one of the biggest American industries of all: Hollywood.

As compared with Rockwell, Warhol's work reminds us that a recognizable rendering of the citizen inside his community has become largely impossible because for all practical purposes the individual himself has ceased to exist. He has been usurped by the corporate "person." This seems to have been the real message and prophetic genius behind Warhol's controversial work.

Rockwell's celebrated paintings, on the other hand, remind us that there is, or rather should be, something beautiful, something intrinsic, something more substantial than mere corporate activity at work inside our numerous neighborhoods. For Rockwell, it was desirable to be a "sentimental realist" simply because the reality before him was so worthy of reproduction. His world was invigorated with the magical elixir called life. The individual—as opposed to the mass-produced products and celebrities from the corporate factory—was still the unrivaled champion of the community. Rockwell's greatest achievement was that he demonstrated, with profound sensitivity and compassion, the overarching personality of man, as opposed to the business venture, dynamically projecting itself within his community.

In every American city, the human actor is overshadowed by the "personhood" of the corporation to an unacceptable degree. This is painfully obvious in everything from the names of our sports stadiums, to the type of music we listen to. Here is one jaded sportswriter commenting on the name of the New York Mets' new stadium, Citi Field, formerly known as Shea Stadium: "Up until now, New York teams had avoided the scourge of corporate naming-rights deals. Let other cities have their FedEx Forums, their Qualcomm Stadiums, their Xcel Energy Centers....We had Madison Square Garden, Yankee Stadium, Giants Stadium and Shea. No need for that corporate nonsense here....[T]hat's why I'll miss the name of Shea Stadium, a name that rolled nicely off the tongue...and was bestowed as an honor for a guy who truly deserved it, with no money changing hands. Imagine that."[149] Most people have a natural need to escape from the demands of commercialism and capitalism, which bombard us 24/7 with messages from every available space. Sports and entertainment (should) offer a form of escapism for people to forget about the daily demands of making a living. The last thing we want when we go to a sporting event is to be reminded about business, the workplace, and the incessant compulsion to earn and spend. Entertainment exists as a pressure-release valve. When the spectators see the profit motive behind the event, the game immediately loses its meaning and purpose.

On a slightly different note, when was the last time a modern musical band produced a noteworthy antiwar song? In just the past decade, America has participated in two major wars (in Iraq and Afghanistan, and a "minor" conflict in Libya), yet it seems as though our musical artists have all gone AWOL.[150] What have so-called artists, such as Lady Gaga, Katy Perry, and Taylor Swift, for example, contributed to the cultural scene aside from sensationalism and depravity? Or how about Madonna's performance at the Pepsi Center in Denver, Colorado, where she brandished a gun at audience members after stepping on a crucifix laying on the stage.[151] Certainly the pop diva had read the reports about one James Holmes, who walked into a screening of "The Dark Knight Rises" and sprayed the audience with automatic gunfire, killing 12 people and injuring dozens more. The massacre happened just days before the Madonna concert in the nearby town of Aurora. If these sort of mindless corporate sell-outs, whom social critic Camille Paglia has referred to as "insipid, bleached-out

---

149 Paul Lukas, "What's in a Name?" *Uni7 Watch*, April 13, 2009.
150 The Vietnam War, for example, was the inspiration for dozens of antiwar songs, including "Give Peace a Chance," 1969, John Lennon; "Saigon Bride," 1967, Joan Baez; "All Along the Watchtower," 1967, Bob Dylan, and covered by Jimi Hendrix, 1968; "Fortunate Son," 1969, Creedence Clearwater Revival; "Leaving on a Jet Plane," 1969, Peter, Paul and Mary; "The Unknown Soldier," 1968, The Doors; "The Grave," 1971, Don McLean; "Gimme Shelter," 1969, The Rolling Stones; "Hello Vietnam," 1965, Johnnie Wright; "People, Let's Stop the War," 1971, Grand Funk Railroad.
151 David Codrea, "Madonna Denver Stage Stunt Shows Hypocrisy and Worse on Guns," *Examiner.com*, October 21, 2012.

personas,"[152] were not dominating the cultural scene, local-born talent would blossom and aspire to something higher, something that the members of the community could readily relate to. Modern performers are providing little more vacuous acts of depravity and perversity for the sake of increased consumer sales dressed up like art. The people want and need more.

Back to Rockwell. His critics tend to view him as a teary-eyed sentimentalist, or a dull realist who failed to see below the surface of things. In fact, nothing could be further from the truth. Norman Rockwell, without getting lost in modernistic, abstract interpretations, had a natural appreciation for the millions of individual threads that hold together the colorful American quilt. Rockwell was simply responding to and portraying the reality of his social environ as it presented itself to him, which, incidentally, provides historians a more accurate portrayal of America's "golden age" than anything the world of academia could hope to achieve. According to one writer, Rockwell's works "project a sense of decencies expected from that part of the foundation for any civil society. The vast Rockwell constituency appreciated loving and respectful human relations."[153] Now it is our duty to determine exactly what has led to the disintegration of decent human relations.

INVASION OF CIRCUS MAXIMUS

In an effort to understand what has led to the disintegration of "loving and respectful human relations" in America that Norman Rockwell depicted in his many paintings, we must consider the state of formal education, for no other institution has more direct influence on our children and society.[154] Education, however, is an

---

152 Camille Paglia, "Taylor Swift, Katy Perry and Hollywood are Ruining Women," *The Hollywood Reporter*, December 6, 2012.

153 Hennessey and Knutson, *Norman Rockwell*, 141.

154 In order to understand the *real* power of education, consider what quickly follows the defeat of a particular state ideology (e.g., communism under the Soviet Union, which was vanquished by the free market creed). "A real revolution," wrote Alexander Herzen, "could only succeed after a process of education and preparation." The new representatives of the

ambiguous concept and, against our popular notions, occurs least of all inside the classroom. The "learning experience" is a lifelong process.

It is the most basic biological fact that all life forms are influenced by their environments. Even the newborn baby immediately recognizes the voice of its parents due to a nine-month-long learning process that occurs inside the womb. And long after individuals complete their formal educational process, life continues to provide invaluable lessons well into old age. Along this bumpy and unpredictable road of learning, it becomes the responsibility of the older generation to pass along the torch of experience, knowledge, and wisdom to the younger generation, thus completing a crucial link between past and future.

"In times gone by," writes Umberto Eco, novelist and professor of semiotics, "the elders were considered the wisest of the tribe, and their task was to pass on their wisdom to their children and grandchildren."[155] Thus, any disruption in the chain of accumulated wisdom, experience, and knowledge would ultimately spell disaster for the civilization in question. Yet that is exactly what is happening in American society, as the fragile tree of knowledge and wisdom is being overwhelmed by the ubiquitous entertainment industry. Indeed, this huge sector of the economy now enjoys more direct influence over the hearts and minds of our children than any teacher, parent, or community leader.

As society surrenders its rightful authority and influence over the lives of its children, corporate power—in various costumes and disguises—enters the scene to fill the void. Today, the entertainment-industrial complex is trampling on highly sensitive terrain— private property, if you will—and is wielding disproportionate influence over the hearts and minds of our youth. This is "private property" in the highest sense of the term, and may be considered as nothing less than illegal trespassing.

new state immediately set about the task of totally revamping the educational system—new textbooks, new allegiances, and new beliefs. The hearts and minds of the new generation must be won before the foundation of a new ideology can be laid.

155   Umberto Eco, *Turning Back the Clock* (London: Vintage, 2008), 359.

Entertainment, however, like technology in general, is not an inherently negative thing. Indeed, life would quickly become unbearable without some form of amusement to dull the edge of urban living, while some form of amusement serves as an acceptable means of escape from the tedious trials and tribulations of making a daily living. No other people in modern history understood this better than the Romans, who lived for bread and circuses. Consider the following description of a festival hosted by Julius Caesar after one of his victorious military campaigns: "When the last triumph had been celebrated, the populace were entertained at a feast for which 22,000 tables were laid, and after it Caesar was escorted to his house by the people and 20 elephants carrying torch-bearers. On the following days the populace were amused with spectacles of every kind. Four hundred lions were hunted to death in the Circus, and not only did gladiators fight each other individually, but also in groups. A naval battle was staged on a tract of the Campus Martius, flooded for the occasion; and as a grand finale, in the Circus Maximus two armies composed of war captives and condemned criminals—1,000 foot, 200 horse, and 20 elephant on either side—fought each other to the death."[156]

It would be difficult to name a modern-day spectacle that could compare with the size and depravity of the abovementioned festival. Yes, the Romans were certainly notorious revelers. But there is a noticeable difference between entertainment in the Roman days and entertainment today, and that is the sheer prevalence of the latter. After all, despite the Romans' well-known appetite for the lewd and outrageous, the abovementioned celebration was not something the average citizen could tolerate each day. And despite Caesar's tremendous wealth, amassed after many years of brutal military campaigns, such extravagant events occurred once or twice in a lifetime. The difference between the ancient Romans and modern society is that entertainment—greatly enhanced by the manipulation of high technology—has become an omnipresent part of the modern landscape.

---

156 Major General J. F. C. Fuller, *Julius Caesar: Man, Soldier & Tyrant* (London: Woodsworth Editions, 1965), 284–285.

Entertainment no longer serves as a temporary escape from the strenuous demands of modern living; indeed, the pursuit of entertainment is arguably the primary reason for the existence of democracy, if not the very definition of democracy: the instantaneous gratification of wants and desires, largely underwritten by the entertainment-industrial complex of the Western world. "Media usage has become more than a supplement to our American lifestyle," writes Professor Jeffrey McCall, "it has become perhaps the largest aspect of our lifestyle." According to McCall, this is regrettable because the "productive pursuits like exercise, family interaction, community work, and household duties are overlooked in order to keep up with *American Idol* or catch the big ball game on TV."[157]

Even faraway battlefields, where an increasing number of US soldiers are now serving, have become pay-per-view spectacles, where the front line is as easily accessible as our living rooms. Who needs gladiatorial battles to quench our thirst for exhilaration when we can experience all the thrill of a real-life battlefield inside the comfort of our homes? When the excitement wanes, as it always does, we casually click to another channel, or perhaps opt to play any number of bloodthirsty video games now available. This onslaught of electronic stimulation challenges our abilities for maintaining a civil society dedicated to human excellence through the pursuit of diligent study and quiet contemplation. Indeed, it is the perfect formula for achieving exactly the opposite effect.

Today, a small group of industry leaders has the unprecedented power to lead children—and with them, the world—astray down the back alleys of society for no other reason than self-enrichment. Or, as Karl Mannheim argued, the elite have perfected the art of "manipulating crowds without which it is impossible to get on in mass-democracies."[158] It has become necessary to intentionally distract and deceive the very individuals who were meant to benefit from democratic government. Thanks to this entertainment-drenched

---

157 Jeffrey McCall, *Viewer Discretion Advised* (Lanham, Maryland: Rowman & Littlefield, 2007), 1.

158 Karl Mannheim, *Ideology and Utopia: An Introduction to the Sociology of Knowledge* (New York: Hartcourt, Brace and Co., 1936), 99.

social engineering, which must constantly work behind the scenes to prevent our mass democracies from unraveling into mass hysteria, we are rapidly on our way to fulfilling Norman Mailer's startling prediction that "the psychopath might very well become the dominant personality in the near future." Modern research is bearing out this prediction.

In a study conducted by Indiana University,[159] it was determined that 92 percent of the top fifty television programs for children between the ages of two and eleven showed characters involved in some form of social aggression. "Social aggression was more likely to be enacted by an attractive perpetrator, to be featured in a humorous context, and neither rewarded or punished," wrote Nicole Martins, assistant professor of telecommunications in the Indiana University College of Arts and Sciences. "In these ways, social aggression on television poses more of a risk for imitation and learning than do portrayals of physical aggression."

The researchers found that, on average, there were fourteen different incidents of social aggression per hour, or once every four minutes. In a nutshell, that is the definition of brainwashing on a mass scale.

Given such a bombardment of negative messages begins practically at birth, it should come as no surprise that our children are behaving antisocially—even those from seemingly respectable backgrounds. In June 2012, an Internet video depicting students from Greece, New York, aboard a school bus verbally abusing a bus monitor, Karen Klein, went viral. Although modern technology helps to sow the seeds of our increasingly coarse culture, in this case it caught the juvenile perpetrators red-handed. While one of the boys filmed the action with his mobile phone, his classmates set upon Klein with a torrent of foul-mouthed language that would have made a hardened convict blush.

An editorial in the local newspaper lamented that the bullying set a "new low in coarse culture."[160] The paper warned that if "this

---

159 Nicole Martins and Barbara J. Wilson, "Mean on the Screen: Social Aggression in Programs Popular with Children," *Journal of Communication*, March 2012.
160 "Greece School Bus Bullying a New Low in Coarse Culture," *Democrat and Chronicle*, June 21, 2012.

episode doesn't shake the community into reassessing its apathy regarding disrespectful and abusive behavior, the community may by beyond repair." The editorial then pointed the finger of blame at the entertainment industry, the one American institution that has found a way to avoid any and all blame when it comes to the destruction of American morals and standards. "How can adults expect children to behave any better than the role models they see at every turn?" the newspaper asked. "It's time to make better choices. From defining expectations in terms of behavior and respect for children, to simply being selective in our choices of music and movies...adults must set a positive example."

The only problem with that advice, however, is that adults today are confronting forces that have grown far beyond their means to control. Most parents and adults, when asked, say they want the world of entertainment to produce more socially responsible products. But the industry, for reasons that remain unknown, refuses to change its dumbing-down strategy. Crass entertainment that breeds crass behavior somehow translates into bigger receipts at the checkout line, it believes, while never giving a moment's thought to the unsustainable cost this implies for society at large.

SPONGEBOB SQUAREPANTS: LUNATIC BABYSITTER

Since television consumes a vast amount of our "community time," it is necessary to consider what kind of corporate programming our children are receiving on a daily basis. Although many parents are perceptive to the problems with today's cartoons, filled as they are with violence and adult humor, millions of other adults never take the time to scrutinize what their kids are watching.

Consider, for example, *SpongeBob SquarePants*, or the adorable, filthy-mouthed characters of *South Park*, or the complete and utter inanity of MTV's *Reality Show*, where the misguided guests seem to have just one lewd thing on their minds night after night after night. (Does anybody actually commit themselves to their homework assignments or household chores in the sex-obsessed world of virtual reality?) In many cases, the very titles of these programs serve to preclude any serious discussion about their inherent worth from the start. How is it possible, for example, to critique a show with the ridiculous name *SpongeBob SquarePants?* The more deranged the production, it seems, the more difficult it becomes to seriously debate the content, which is probably why so many otherwise intelligent parents believe that such programming is innocent and harmless. That is, until now.

A comprehensive study that appeared in *Pediatrics,* the official journal of the American Academy of Pediatrics,[161] demonstrated the effects of "fast-paced cartoons" on children's behavior. The methodology of the test was as follows: Sixty four-year-olds were randomly assigned to one of three conditions (twenty children each): fast-paced television, educational television, or drawing. The fast-paced television group watched a nine-minute segment of a "very popular fantastical cartoon about an animated sponge that lives under the sea." The educational television group watched a nine-minute segment of a realistic Public Broadcasting Service cartoon about a "typical US preschool-aged boy." The remaining children were given markers and crayons to draw. The conclusion of the study has been described as significant: Based on a series of tests given to the sixty children following their activities, the group that watched the fast-paced television fared the worst. According to the researchers, "Just 9 minutes of viewing a fast-paced television cartoon had immediate negative effects on 4-year-olds' executive function."[162]

The golden age of animation sprung to life thanks to the prolific genius of Walt Disney, who introduced American television audiences to a vast array of wholesome and endearing characters, such as Mickey Mouse, Snow White and the Seven Dwarfs, Three

---

161 Angeline S. Lillard and Jennifer Peterson, "The Immediate Impact of Different Types of Television on Young Children's Executive Function," *Pediatrics,* September 12, 2011. To read the study in its entirety: http://pediatrics.aappublications.org/content/early/2011/09/08/peds.2010–1919.

162 Ibid. Note: "Executive function" is described in the study as "key to positive social and cognitive functioning and is strongly associated with success in school."

Little Pigs, Pinocchio, Steamboat Willie, and Bambi. What parent would be apprehensive about allowing children to watch such first-rate productions? Who would feel pangs of guilt about leaving children temporarily in the hands of such a responsible caregiver? Today, with both parents employed and the children home alone, this is no moot point. Although there is always a temptation to exaggerate the wholesomeness and goodness of times gone by, it is obvious that the content and professional quality of modern productions fare very poorly next to their golden antecedents.

A noticeable decline in cartoon content and design was brought about thanks to Nickelodeon, which introduced the positively deranged cartoon *The Ren & Stimpy Show* in 1988. For those unfamiliar with these two characters, imagine Wile E. Coyote and the Road Runner on cocaine. Any effort to describe these characters, which exhibit personality disorders that could be described only as psychotic, would fail to do them justice. (The artistic genius behind this animation revolution, John Kricfalusi, went on to create a number of other brilliant role models for criminal behavior, including *Jimmy the Idiot Boy, Rugrats,* and *The Goddamn George Liquor Program.* And who could ever forget *Weekend Pussy Hunt,* a completely demented and deranged, made-for-Internet production that attracted a large number of children viewers?) Meanwhile, the hyperactive tempo of these shows, which bounces frantically from frame to frame, leaves the viewer feeling almost nauseous, a bit like trying to play a video game inside a moving vehicle. Little wonder that kids must be medicated (courtesy of the corporate pharmaceuticals, of course) just to sit still in the classroom these days.

Or consider MTV, which started in 1981 as a channel devoted to playing music videos. Today, the channel has transformed into a cultural train wreck that specializes in peddling to young audiences the lowest form of vulgarity. Here are just some of the show titles, which practically require no explanation: *Jersey Shore* (a "bordello-like house set," said an Italian rights organization[163]), *Ridiculousness* (rated TV-PG for language and violence), *16 and Pregnant*

---

163 "'Italian-Americans Slam 'Jersey Shore,'" UPI, December 4, 2009.

(go figure), *Beavis and Butt-head* (yet more evidence that adults think they can present anything so long as it is in the form of a cartoon character), *Jackass* (the name says it all), and a multitude of "reality" shows that are saturated in sex-based themes.

In a one-week period (March 20, 2004, to March 27, 2004), the Parents Television Council (PTC) performed content analysis of MTV programming during its popular annual "Spring Break" coverage. "In 171 hours of MTV programming, PTC analysts found a staggering 1,548 sexual scenes containing 3,056 depictions of sex and various forms of nudity and 2,881 verbal sexual references. That means that children watching MTV are viewing an average of 9 sexual scenes per hour with approximately 18 sexual depictions and 17 instances of sexual dialogue and innuendo."[164] Concerning the trash-filled reality programs, the PTC reported: "In 66 hours of reality programming, PTC analysts recorded 833 segments containing sexual content, or 12.6 scenes per hour. Within those 833 segments, there were 905 visual depictions of sexual activity and 917 verbal references."[165]

It is important to note, however, that there have been victories against the US media titans, who are constantly pushing the envelope when it comes to culturally explosive issues. MTV, for example, a unit of Viacom, and the creators of wonderfully vacuous trash, like "The Real World" and "Jersey Shore," recently terminated one of its shows due to a public outcry. The show, titled 'Skins,' which was aimed directly at the teenage viewer, delved so deep into issues of promiscuity, drugs, and homosexuality that critics slammed it as pornographic."

"In one episode, a naked 17-year-old actor is shown from behind as he runs down a street. The actor, Jesse Carere, plays Chris, a high school student whose erection — assisted by erectile dysfunction pills — is a punch line throughout the episode."[166] Does anybody recall when MTV actually played music videos?

---

164 Casey Williams, "MTV Smut Peddlers," Parents Television Council, 2005, 3.
165 Ibid, 4.
166 Brian Stelter, "A Racy Show with Teenagers Steps Back from a Boundary," *New York Times*, January 19, 2011.

The Parents Television Council (PTC) called on the chairmen of the US Senate and House Judiciary committees and the Department of Justice to open investigations into what the PTC alleges is child pornography on the MTV program involving young actors, some of whom are below the age of 16. The PTC has 1.3 million members. Eventually MTV was forced to yank the show, but only after advertisers started distancing themselves from the uproar.

The demise of the golden age of American television and the rise of something utterly degenerate and unrecognizable becomes more of an issue when we recall how much time our children are influenced by this single medium. "A television is on somewhere in the American home about eight hours per day," writes Jeffrey McCall, before rattling off a whole list of disturbing statistics. "Each person in the home watches television an average of about four hours per day. Even kids six years of age and younger watch television almost two hours per day, according to recent research by the Kaiser Family Foundation."[167] Meanwhile, research compiled from Nielson Media Research shows that the average American home "has more televisions than people."[168] Considering that, in addition to the increasingly disturbing content available at the push of a button, "[T]he average child in America will view over forty thousand television commercials each year," we have considerable reason for concern. Indeed, in light of television's unmatched influence—greater than that of parents, greater than that of teachers—there is no excuse for the entertainment industry flooding the airwaves with garbage. Yet that is exactly what is happening.

The corporate world reflexively responds to its critics that it is only giving the consumers what they want—the classic "market-driven morality" defense where nobody is to blame but the hidden hand of the economy. We are only responding, industry members cry, to the desires of the consumers (who are also known, we must add, to stop and stare at horrible traffic accidents on their way to the shopping mall). But if this were really true, then we would still be holding gladiatorial matches inside stadiums because "that is

---

167 McCall, *Viewer Discretion Advised*, 103; statistic on children and commercials, 107.
168 Ibid, 108.

what the people wanted." Eventually, it was Caesar himself who put a stop to the senseless slaughter in the public square.

Today, we mindlessly permit corporations to set the standards—which include psychological standards, as well as the artistic—to determine what is permissible for children and adolescents to watch on television and in the theaters. And why does it seem that the more depraved programs regularly get top billing? Is it really simply a case of responding to the market impulses of our little darlings, who demand to be spoon-fed a daily dose of violence-saturated and moronic programs? And if it turns out to be true that our children are more transfixed by disturbing and violent images, as opposed to the more wholesome productions, don't the adults have the right, indeed, the duty, to step in and assert their guidance and good sense?

The lightning advance of technology guarantees that every form of entertainment is omnipresent and inescapable; the joystick is on demand 24/7. Unless we expect our children to live in hermetically sealed environments, it remains altogether impossible to shield them from the powerful influence of the modern entertainment mill. Given the omnipresence of entertainment in combination with the Internet (available on handheld devices now), it has become virtually impossible to shield kids from loaded messages, including sex, murder, and violence. But let's suppose that an island of tranquillity does exist where children could be safely isolated from the degenerate message of modern entertainment. What then? Eventually, they would have to deal with the consequences of a morally bankrupt society. In other words, "isolating" ourselves and our children from these degenerate forms of entertainment will not protect us; it will only give us a temporary sense of victory. The onus is on our business and political leaders to understand that an ignorant populace is more dangerous to the ruling bodies than an enlightened, well-educated one.

With each passing generation, however, the decision makers become more willing to accept puerile entertainment. This is a tragedy in the making. By remaining indifferent to what messages our children are receiving, the fragile link between student and teacher is being unforgivably severed. That we now ignore the importance of these human links to the past—the vital springs of all wisdom—can be seen through our predilection for abandoning the elderly—the *senior citizens*—in nursing facilities, while attempting to download the *facts* of history—never mind *wisdom*—through the bloodless hardware of the Internet.

Tragically, the Circus Maximus is not a place we visit on rare occasions as the Romans did. The Circus Maximus has become our very living rooms. Electricity instantaneously delivers the action into our homes and hands every second of every day, nonstop, whenever and wherever we summon the entertainment genie. When we are not home, the entertainment is readily portable. While the social implications of these "modern conveniences" are mind-boggling and impossible to fully measure, the ultimate consequence they have on the development of our youth is easy to predict, especially when the evidence is readily available through the behavior of our children.[169] But not everybody, of course, views these disturbing cultural trends as a negative phenomenon.

Zbigniew Brzezinski, the national security adviser to President Jimmy Carter from 1977 to 1981, gave an apologetic defense of America's "hedonistic" mass culture that has taken the entire world by storm: "Cultural domination has been an underappreciated facet of American global power. Whatever one may think of its aesthetic values, America's mass culture exercises a magnetic appeal, especially on the world's youth. Its attraction may be derived from the hedonistic quality of the lifestyle it projects, but its global appeal is undeniable. American television programs and films account for about three-fourths of the global market. American popular music is equally dominant, while American

---

169 To understand the dreadful state of Western education, consider the Third International Mathematics and Science Study, billed as the most comprehensive international study of academic achievement ever. In a twenty-one-nation test of general high school math skills, US twelfth-graders ranked nineteenth, outperforming only Cyprus and lowest-ranking South Africa. In a similar twenty-one-nation test of general high school science knowledge, US twelfth-graders ranked sixteenth, outperforming only five other Third World nations. Science students in the United States ranked last in a sixteen-nation physics test.

fads, eating habits, and even clothing are increasingly imitated worldwide."[170]

Brzezinski casually accepts the "hedonistic quality" of modern entertainment, because it has broad "global appeal" that entrenches America's "cultural domination" around the globe; as with so many other things American these days, it is not the quality of the product that matters, but the sheer size, quantity, and marketability. In other words, why should we care about "aesthetic values" when the really important matter, at least for those selling tickets to this show, is "cultural domination."

Ironically, American conservatives like Brzezinski erroneously believe that it is their political ideology that offers society a safe haven from the selfish liberal creed. The fact is, however, both political ideologies, liberal and conservative alike, are firmly anchored to the corporate bandwagon. The liberals, who believe wholeheartedly in the freedom of expression, tend to promote, or at least support, any degenerate message that shocks the senses and challenges the stagnant status quo (which is somehow misconstrued as being the real definition of art and even freedom these days). The conservatives, meanwhile, feign to despise the deranged genre, which they probably do, but begrudgingly turn a blind eye because it fattens their pocketbooks.

The ironic collaboration between the American conservatives and liberals became apparent when film director Michael Moore visited a Kmart store in his movie *Bowling for Columbine* and demanded it stop selling bullets (in protest to the Columbine school massacre, where two adolescents went on a shooting spree, killing fifteen). Support of the Second Amendment right to bear arms is a well-known keystone in conservative philosophy. Moore went on to chastise Charlton Heston, the former head of the National Rifle Association, America's most powerful congressional lobby, inside Heston's own home. The film director and social critic, however, did not distribute the blame fairly and equally.

---

170   Zbigniew Brzezinski, *The Grand Chessboard* (New York: HarperCollins Publishers, 1997), 25.

Moore failed to find fault with violent video games and Hollywood movies, for example, forms of artistic expression sacred to liberals, which the two Columbine gunmen frequently indulged in prior to their killing spree. Moreover, in comparison with his tough talk with the head of the NRA, Moore expressed sympathy and almost compassion for shock rocker Marilyn Manson, whose depraved song lyrics seem to have played at least a partial influence on the actions of the two high school killers. The overt message that Moore provides is that the conservative party provides the ammunition, so to speak, that kill our youth. At the same time, however, he ignores the possibility that it is the liberals who instill the deadly message that is not so readily visible as a box of bullets. A person who has been raised in an atmosphere of sound cultural influences will not present a threat to his or her fellow citizens.

Moore's film, however, does make one critical point: The Columbine shooting took place on April 20, 1999, which happened to be the "largest one-day bombing by the US in the Kosovo war." Moore begins by showing then-President Bill Clinton at a news conference where he was attempting to rationalize the attack and "minimize harm to innocent people." That was, however, a difficult goal to achieve considering that "on the hit list were a local hospital and primary school." Moore then segues into the Columbine tragedy. On the screen flashes the headline "One Hour Later." One hour after announcing the fierce bombing of a Serbian village, Clinton announces: "We all know there has been a terrible shooting at a high school in Littleton, Colorado."

According to Carl Savich, "Moore's central thesis is that there is a direct link between the US murders of Serbian civilians and the murders of Columbine High School. To understand the former you have to understand the latter. And to explain both, you have to understand US foreign policy during the Cold War and the American culture of violence, a gun culture rooted in racial paranoia and fear."[171]

---

171 Carl Savich, "Kosovo and Columbine: Kosovo in Context," *Serbianna*, September 26, 2006.

THE IMPORTANCE OF AN (UNINTERRUPTED) EDUCATION

The ignorance of the masses can no longer be taken for granted. The world has become too dangerous and volatile a place for the toleration, not to mention propagation, of idiocy; our freedom and liberty can no longer give sanction to disorder and anarchy. The education of our children is a delicate process that cannot tolerate outside distractions. Despite the tremendous short-term advantages to a globalized economy that an ignorant populace permits, these advantages quickly transform into dangerous liabilities that no nation, however powerful, can withstand for long. As Thomas Jefferson aptly stated in a letter (dated January 6, 1816) to Colonel Charles Yancey: "*If a nation expects to be ignorant and free, in a state of civilization, it expects what never was and never will be.*"

Indeed, the best investment for any nation is to provide for a well-educated citizenry. Yet America somehow finds it more logical to invest in state-of-the-art prisons as opposed to a state-of-the-art school system. And when all else fails, we have recourse to capital punishment. It would be far better if we worked to instill strong values into the hearts and minds of our youth, as opposed to attempting to remedy them after they have already gone astray. "Human nature is not a machine," wrote John Stuart Mill in his famous treatise *On Liberty*, that is "to be built after a model, and set to do exactly the work prescribed for it, but a tree, which requires to grow and develop itself on all sides, according to the tendency of the inward forces which make it a living thing."

And when the "inward forces" of man is understood to be the most valuable possession, which demands to be cared for with the greatest care, only then will man rise up to his greatest stature. He will fulfil the ancient Greek requirement for attaining the highest level of maturity: *gnothi seauton,* "Know thyself."

When man is filled with the beauty of poetry, the perfection of geometry, and the wisdom of history, when he is enraptured with music, calmed by literature, and humbled by wisdom, only then will he be a man truly worthy of the name. A government unto himself who will, by the strength and grace of his tempered intelligence, work to remove any attempts at subjugation and corruption at his expense. The executive, legislative, and judicial branches of government will shine in his soul and be reflected in a superior countenance. "There's no art," King Duncan commented in Shakespeare's play *Macbeth,* "to find the mind's construction in the face." Intelligence is a marked trait every bit as much as physical beauty. It also prevents the people from suffering abuse at the hands of other men.

An enlightened man *will* permit others to rule on his behalf, but should this rule become tyrannical, should his representatives forget their primary duty to the people, then he will possess the moral and intellectual capacities for immediately confronting the threat as he deems necessary and just. Therefore, in order for humans to aspire to the highest level of their potentialities, and thus help the nation to right itself in times of upheaval and duress, all men and women must be given the educational tools for becoming a government unto themselves. The universe and university are inside each person, and only a social commitment to discover this innate power will set man free.

However, such intimate knowledge of the self would disrupt the present socioeconomic paradigm, which demands insecure, self-conscious, and distracted consumers, as opposed to a strong and enlightened citizenry. As it stands, the global village is being subjected to a corporate barrage of commercialism, which educates the global youth to behave only as mindless consumers. Consider this article from the *Wall Street Journal,* which captures the essence of these commercially saturated times.

> MUNICH—In a bid to be more hip
> and less patronizing, McDonald's Corp.
> launched a global marketing campaign
> featuring a set of MTV-style commercials
> and a jingle with vocals provided by U.S.
> star Justin Timberlake.
> At a night club here, McDonald's

> screened three of the five commercials
> the chain will show around the world
> with its new slogan, "I'm Lovin' It." Set
> to a pop song theme, the fast-paced
> commercials aim to sell youth and fun
> rather than just a meal with the family.[172]

A civilized society cannot continue to be pummelled by such inane notions, where fast food, nightclubs, and MTV are permitted to substitute for "just a meal with the family." Just like that, a two-thousand-year Western tradition is wiped out in favor of a hamburger-hawking clown; the "experience" of fast food takes precedent over a slow, thoughtful dinner with the family. We have handed corporate America carte blanche powers in altering every aspect of our society, right down to the once-solemn family dinner.

Perhaps it should come as no surprise that the only US corporations that saw their stock prices rise in 2008, the year of the Great Recession, were the two companies that have become metaphors for corporate recklessness: Wal-Mart and McDonald's.

HOW DID AMERICA BECOME OBESE?

Although it may sound overly simplistic to say that we Americans have grown soft on a steady diet of 24/7 capitalist comforts, there is no escaping some ugly truths. For example, obesity rates are soaring in the land of the free, as are cases of Type 2 Diabetes, which has tripled among US children in the past 30 years. According to the Centers for Disease Control and Prevention (CDC), more than one-third of US adults (35.7%) are obese – a 12 % increase since 2000. Meanwhile, soda drinks and sweetened beverages now rank as the number-one source of calories in the American diet.

---

172 "McDonald's Youth Movement: Ad Blitz Targets a Hipper Crowd," *Wall Street Journal*, September 3, 2003.

Today, tens of thousands of fast-food outlets have wreaked a very real violence on our communities, not to mention our waistlines. "Eating out" is no longer a once-in-a-while event; it has become a way of life (sometime in the near future, we will probably see the fast-food industry bogged down in the next big American legal battle, much like the cigarette industry experienced at the beginning of the decade). These ubiquitous eating establishments, which dominate the roadsides of just about every US town and city, are helping to promote high levels of obesity among all members of society.

The CDC, which compiled obesity-rate "maps" of the fifty US states for every year between 1985 and 2008, shows breathtaking lcaps in obesity rates in this very brief period. In 1985, the average obesity rate per state was about 10 percent, while many states, such as California, New York, and Florida, registered less than that amount. By 1995, the CDC obesity map was beginning to reveal new colors, as not a single state fell into the 10-percent-or-less category. Middle America, which had fallen into the 10–14 percent range, was now predominantly dark blue. Ten years later, in 2005, the map was no longer recognizable by its original color makeup. Previously unheard of orange and red states, which indicated obesity rates in the 20–30 percent neighborhood, almost completely dominated the country. By 2008, thirty-two states showed obesity rates equal to or greater than 25 percent, while six states (Alabama, Mississippi, Oklahoma, South Carolina, Tennessee, and West Virginia) were screaming red at 30 percent or greater. Colorado, the only dark blue state left on America's obesity map, ranked as the great exception with "just" 18.5 percent of the population obese.[173]

Meanwhile, another study, led by Dr. Gregory Burke, of Wake Forest University, Winston Salem, North Carolina, shows "alarming levels" of obesity in ethnic groups across the board in the United

---

173 Obesity is defined as a body mass index (BMI) of thirty or greater. BMI is calculated from a person's weight and height and provides a reasonable indicator of body fatness and weight categories that may lead to health problems. Obesity is a major risk factor for cardiovascular disease, certain types of cancer, and type 2 diabetes. Adapted from the Centers for Disease Control and Prevention website.

States. "The obesity epidemic has the potential to reduce further gains in U.S. life expectancy, largely through an effect on cardiovascular disease mortality (death)," Burke and his colleagues warn in the *Archives of Internal Medicine* journal. [174]

What is looming on the American horizon is nothing short of a potential catastrophe since obesity, which greatly increases the risk of diabetes, heart disease, and other "silent diseases," is now striking the baby boom generation, placing a huge burden on health care providers, not to mention their clients. But the tragedy goes far beyond our bursting waistlines. Meals today are rarely shared with others but are increasingly consumed in the privacy of one's automobile "on the go." This monopolization and degradation of the sacred dinner, which bears absolutely no resemblance to Rockwell's endearing painting *Family Grace* (1938), continues unimpeded in all other sectors of the American economy. Huge, homogenized, fast, and monopolized is quickly replacing local, unique, slow, and shared; this irreparable loss cuts to the very core of our democratic institutions.

In these fast and furious times, it is easily forgotten that food in general and dinner in particular play a major role in bringing together members of the family. Indeed, dinners may provide the only pretext for members of a family to actually sit down and talk to each other on a daily basis. The sacred event even plays a large role in uniting the country. Yet we have allowed this cherished part of our lives to be largely consumed by industrial farming and the fast-food industry, corporate ventures that have very little understanding as to what comprises a normally functioning society.

"Fast food chains are trying to poach customers from 'casual dining' chains," the *Economist* magazine wrote, "...while those chains are squeezing out independent restaurants unable to compete on cost or in marketing clout. Business conditions...are the real threat to the weaker firms."[175]

Although it is impossible to turn back the hands of time to some fabled Rockwellian gilded age, we may still learn some valu-

---

174   Megan Rauscher, "U.S. Obesity Rates Alarmingly High," Reuters, May 12, 2008.
175   "Thin Pickings," *Economist,* July 14, 2005, 32.

able lessons from what appears to have been a more innocent and spiritually healthier chapter of American history. Although the world today is a dramatically changed place, there is still room for the humility that would allow us to see that we can learn from earlier ages how best to organize our modern societies.

"The fidelity of the citizens to each other and to the state was confirmed by the habits of education and the prejudices of religion," advised a wise Greek named Polybius, who underscored the reasons for the greatness of Rome. "Honour, as well as virtue, was the principle of the republic; the ambitious citizens laboured to deserve the solemn glories of a triumph; and the ardour of the Roman youth was kindled into active emulation as often as they beheld the domestic images of their ancestors."[176] Tragically and inexplicably, the support structure that allows the family unit to stand strong is being deliberately kicked away in favor of corporate ambitions.

A COFFEEHOUSE REVOLUTION?

It should come as no surprise that Starbucks, the multinational chain of coffee shops traded on the Nasdaq, has attracted the wrath of the anti-globalization protesters. After all, coffee shops once represented the front line of social criticism, a place where bohemians, artists, and revolutionaries gathered to discuss their ideas. "In the early part of the eighteenth century," writes Dr. Lewis A. Coser, "there were about 2,000 coffeehouses in London, and every profession, trade and party had its favorite." Coser noted that the existence of these establishments "allowed intellectuals to perform one of their most important tasks: to contribute to the formation of public opinion."[177]

In the brave new America, however, the bearded academics and intellectuals have been practically severed from the community at large and relegated safely in their ivory towers, perform-

---

176 Edward Gibbon, *The Decline and Fall of the Roman Empire* (New York: Viking Press, 1952), 620.

177 Lewis A. Coser, *Men of Ideas* (New York: Free Press Paperbacks, 1997), 23, 25.

ing intensely specialized research—mostly for the sole benefit of corporate power—with government grants that only make them subservient to the politico-corporate will. Thus, the workers have lost their connection to academia as a means of defense.

Originally, the spirit of the entrepreneur—whether he owned a coffee shop or a shoe store—represented the real essence of the political conservatives. Corporate power actually has very little in common with the conservative philosophy besides money, which, as any true conservative understands, does not define the philosophy's core principles or objectives. Conservatism, which in Latin means to "guard and protect," would never concede to the hideous social and cultural disfigurement of our national treasures, symbolized by the cancerous spread of superstores and hypermarkets across our proud land.

Edmund Burke, an outspoken proponent of tradition and "organic" change, argued that the conservative philosophy was a duty "to preserve, and an ability to improve." Historian Will Durant described the purpose of the conservative philosophy as "defending the necessity of religion, the wisdom of tradition, the authority of the family...and the constant need to maintain political, moral, and economic dikes against the ever-swelling sea of popular ignorance, cupidity, violence, barbarism, and fertility."[178]

Leo Tolstoy opened his novel *Anna Karenina* with this famous line: "All happy families are alike but an unhappy family is unhappy after its own fashion." In that Russian author's day, before the world of economics and finance had crystallized into an irresistible global force, a variety of social factors affected each individual family. Today, by comparison, the challenges confronting families are much more predictable.

By surrendering to the laissez-faire acumen of "free market" philosophy, where corporations are the primary individual, politicians no longer have a vested interest in honoring and protecting the family establishment as such. Indeed, to ignore the disintegration of the family unit, each through its own tragic demise, is

---

178 Will and Ariel Durant, *The Age of Napoleon* (New York: Simon and Schuster, 1975), 222.

viewed as a positive growth factor from the marbled halls of the corporate world. The dynamics of globalization and corporate power are making it impossible for the nuclear family, the one faithfully portrayed by Norman Rockwell, to be a successful venture. Yet it is the indispensable family unit that is responsible for nurturing healthy individuals who will one day have the responsibility of governing our state, not to mention our corporations.

Thus, in light of the new realities, we must respectfully amend Tolstoy's quaint adage to the flow of modern events: *An unhappy family is unhappy due to vast economic and political forces that are beyond the ability of traditional democratic procedure to harness.*

CHAPTER V
On the Road to Corporate Tyranny

This culture represents the fulfilment of an old managerial ideal: to exact universal assent, not through outright force, but by creating an environment that would make dissent impossible.

—MARK CRISPIN MILLER

Although rarely discussed in our mainstream news, there is an epic power struggle raging inside the United States that pits the corporate elite against the defenders of democracy. For the elite, the fruits of victory are much more than just the commanding heights of the global economy; it is our entire political system. This raises the simple question: Why do the corporate elite want or need more power? After all, they already enjoy exorbitant salaries, the highest in the free world, while the total value of their earth-straddling companies exceeds that of many sovereign states. Meanwhile, the stock market, despite a floundering labor market, is doing a roaring business. Yet the masters of the universe are still not content. Why do America's business leaders feel the need to control our political process as well? Why must they control the entire game?

Concerning the accumulation of power, one thing is clear: These individuals will never be satisfied, and their thirst for greater influence will never be quenched. That is because the more power and influence a particular group acquires, the more it desires and needs. From a Machiavellian point of view, this is understandable since any group that accumulates excessive authority will soon become the target of suspicion and even loathing from the rest of society, which inherently understands the dangers of one group obtaining absolute powers. The usurpation of power that we are witnessing today, however, is of a far more subtle nature than it was in other periods of history. Today, the battle is occurring without so much as a gunshot behind the locked doors of Congress and the courts, where our government representatives, selling themselves out like cheap whores to corporate lobbyists, have destroyed any notion of democracy.

The infinite wisdom of our sacred Constitution is being undercut by a political system that both defends and is dependent upon corporate power. With the Supreme Court under their wing, our political and corporate overlords are putting as much space between themselves and democratic procedure as possible. The American people, despite some stubborn pockets of resistance, are helpless in the face of this hijacking. At the same time, the journalistic community—members of the so-called Fourth Estate whose job it is to sound the alarm on attacks against civil society—are largely employed by the same corporate forces that are wrecking our society. Aside from a few courageous private ventures, the corporate elite control the entire social and cultural milieu. Through their vast media holdings, they alone decide what is important for public discussion and debate and what is not. They inundate media markets with mindless entertainment—from songs to movies to magazines—that mostly serves to disturb, dumb down, and distract from crucial issues. They remind us repeatedly about the terrorist threat, while the real menace to our society continues to roam Wall Street like a pack of rabid wolves, circling for its next easy kill. The once-proud and self-reliant American people have become so overwhelmed with superfluous issues that they fail to recognize their new masters, the corporate overlords, who happily provide us everything under the sun—including our very opinions—all in order to enslave us.

Meanwhile, as the economic contradictions of our society continue to proliferate, we are moving closer with each passing day to all-out class warfare. Those who think this is an exaggeration (Warren Buffett and George Soros do not) need only consider the heavy paramilitary police presence at every global financial event and the extreme measures being taken to eliminate democratic debate and dissent. Although our corporate and political leaders clearly see that their global agenda is generally repugnant to the majority of people, this does not stop them from attempting to reconstruct the American Dream to conform to the interests of their own limited class. Eventually this boiling cauldron of contradictions, which is conspicuous in its inequality and the disenfranchisement of millions of Americans, must blow its lid unless a new political outlook is permitted to blossom.

CONTROLLING THE GAME

Historians have already demonstrated that political attitudes among the people continuously ebb and flow over time. Like a pendulum, a conservative mood today eventually "swings back" to a more liberal frame of mind tomorrow, and vice versa, in a cycle that will terminate only with the end of history. These epochal episodes, which could be described as the political heartbeat of the nation, have been observed by various historians, including Arthur M. Schlesinger, who neatly summarized the "systole and diastole" of America's political body over the past century. "The private interest of the 1920s had led to the public action of the 1930s, the 1950s now led into the 1960s and a new rush of commitment: Kennedy and the New Frontier; Johnson and the Great Society; the racial revolution, the war on poverty," he observed. "By the later 1970s Americans were once more, as they had been in the 1950s and 1920s, fed up with public action and disenchanted by its consequences. The time received its appropriate names—the 'me' decade; the 'culture of narcissism.' The reaction reached its culmination in the age of Reagan in the 1980s."[179]

The election of Ronald Reagan heralded in a wave of corporate "neoliberalism," a politico-economic philosophy that has come to dominate American politics down to our day irrespective of the political party in power. Indeed, as power gravitated to the corporate giants and their political servants, the gap between the economic haves and have-nots has grown to unprecedented levels. In fact, at practically the same moment that Reagan won the presidency the United States inherited the title as the most unequal industrialized nation. "Since the 1980s, the United States has replaced France as the major nation with the largest gap between the rich and the poor," writes Kevin Phillips. "Wealth and income stratification—the hardening of the economy's arteries—was world-class and worsening."[180] This historic shift was predicated upon the dramatic rise of US corporate power, which no longer had to fear changes in the political climate, the voice of labor, or a social backlash. In short, corporations control the entire game—lock, stock, and barrel.

This radical transformation of American society in general and the economy in particular cannot be solely blamed on the Republican Party or conservative philosophy. After all, the American people continue to experience steep drops in their standard of living rates even when Democratic leaders are in power. Indeed, there is developing a convergence of ideology between the Democrat and Republican camps to such a degree that it is increasingly difficult to distinguish between them and work they perform on behalf of corporations.[181] The result is an increasingly homogeneous political vision that considers the existence of corporate power inside our political system as a natural phenomenon; although a handful of politicians dare to broach the subject, the majority understand

---

179 Arthur M. Schlesinger Jr., *The Cycles of American History* (Boston: Houghton Mifflin Company, 1986), 32.

180 Kevin Phillips, *American Dynasty* (New York: Penguin Books, 2004), 68.

181 Third-party candidates, including Ralph Nader, Ron Paul, Pat Buchanan, and Lyndon LaRouche, are routinely ridiculed and ignored by the US media.

that voicing an opinion that threatens the "liberty and freedom" of corporations is no less hazardous than stepping into a minefield (and all the more so with the recent passage of *Citizens United*). The Democrats and Republicans, fawning defenders of "special interests," heed their masters' call by endorsing a pro-business agenda that is predicated on globalization, deregulation, and the so-called free market.

So now the elite, on the defensive at a time when so many Americans are clamouring for real political change, are doubling up on their defenses and battening down the hatches. The elite want to make sure the people do not succeed in turning the tide against corporate power, replacing it with a more progressive political outlook. They wish to kill any sort of pro-democratic movement in its tracks in order to maintain their iron grip on the economic and political realms. For our immediate purposes, it is important to understand how corporate power came to infest the halls of power in the first place. The simple answer, of course, is money, which the richest Americans are in the position to invest into our political process for their own intensely private gain. The more difficult problem remains an age-old dilemma: how to separate the world of economic special interests from the world of politics.

CORPORATE CONTROL OF US PRESIDENTIAL DEBATES

Many Americans are unfamiliar with the dirtiest little secret concerning the American political process: The US presidential campaigns are literally owned and operated by the Republicans and Democrats, underwritten by American corporations, and packaged under the innocent-sounding title the Commission on Presidential Debates (CPD). The CPD is run by Frank J. Fahrenkopf, a pharmaceutical industry lobbyist, and Michael D. McCurry, the former press secretary for Bill Clinton. Ironically, CPD came into existence because the former organizing committee of the debates was performing its duties too well.

133

Between 1976 and 1984, the independent League of Women Voters organized the US presidential debates. On the eve of the 1988 presidential debates between George H. W. Bush and Michael Dukakis, however, a shocking thing happened: The Democrats and Republicans presented to the League, the very organization that served as the official moderator and organizer, a list of demands as to how the debates would be held! To call this an act of arrogance would fall a bit wide of the mark.

Below is the news release[182] explaining why the league decided to end its affiliation with the presidential debates. The comments, reproduced here in their entirety, provide some nice insight into exactly how ineffectual the election process has become:

NEWS RELEASE
FOR IMMEDIATE RELEASE
October 3, 1988

LEAGUE REFUSES TO "HELP PERPETUATE A FRAUD" WITHDRAWS SUPPORT FROM FINAL PRESIDENTIAL DEBATE

WASHINGTON, D.C. — "The League of Women Voters is withdrawing its sponsorship of the presidential debate scheduled for mid-October because the demands of the two campaign organizations [the Democrats and the Republicans] would perpetrate a fraud on the American voter," League President Nancy M. Neuman said today.

"It has become clear to us that the candidates' organizations aim to add debates to their list of campaign-trail charades devoid of substance, spontaneity and honest answers to tough questions," Neuman said. "The League has no intention of becoming an accessory to the hoodwinking of the American public."

---

182 News release available at the League of Women Voters website: www.lwv.org/press-release/league-refuses-help-perpetuate-fraud.

Neuman said that the campaigns presented the League with their debate agreement…two weeks before the scheduled debate. The campaigns' agreement was negotiated "behind closed doors" and was presented to the league as "a done deal," she said, its 16 pages of conditions not subject to negotiation.

Most objectionable to the League, Neuman said, were conditions in the agreement that gave the campaigns unprecedented control over the proceedings. Neuman called "outrageous" the campaigns' demands that they control the selection of questioners, the composition of the audience, hall access for the press and other issues.

"The campaigns' agreement is a closed-door masterpiece," Neuman said. "Never in the history of the league of Woman Voters have two candidates' organizations come to us with such stringent, unyielding and self-serving demands."

Neuman said she and the League regretted that the American people have had no real opportunities to judge the presidential nominees outside of campaign-controlled environments.

"On the threshold of a new millennium, this country remains the brightest hope for all who cherish free speech and open debate," Neuman said. "Americans deserve to see and hear the men who would be president face each other in a debate on the hard and complex issues critical to our progress into the next century."

It needs to be stressed that the league, as an outside, impartial sponsor of the presidential debates, ensured that all political hopefuls had a fair chance of having their voices heard. That is no longer the case. Connie Rice, the civil rights activist and lawyer, said the league "ran these debates with an iron hand as open, transparent, nonpartisan events."[183] As Rice explains: "The men running the major campaigns ended (the League of Women Voters) control

---

183 Connie Rice, "Top 10 Secrets They Don't Want You to Know about the Debates," NPR, September 29, 2004.

when the league defiantly included John Anderson and Ross Perot and used tough moderators and formats the parties didn't like. The (Democrats and Republicans) snatched the debates from the league and formed the Commission on Presidential Debates—the CPD—in 1986."

For those hoping that the US presidential debate stage may one day find extra space to host a third-party candidate, better not hold your breath. Those illusions were shattered when Ross Perot, who received just under 19 percent of the popular vote (approximately twenty million votes) in the 1992 election, was barred from participating in the presidential debates four years later. The CPD had the supreme audacity to claim that Perot should be excluded from the presidential debates because he had "no realistic chance of winning." An editorial in the *New York Times* summed up the frustration felt by millions of cheated voters: "By deciding yesterday to exclude Ross Perot from this year's debates, the commission proved itself to be a tool of the two dominant parties rather than a guardian of the public interest. This commission has no legal standing to monopolize debates, and it is time for some more fair-minded group to get into the business of sponsoring these important events."[184]

Today, the Democrat- and Republican-controlled CPD has cornered the market on the debate process, and, by extension, the entire election process as well. In order to be considered eligible to participate in the debates, candidates are required to prove they have the support of at least 15 percent of the electorate, which is determined by five national public opinion polling organizations. This presents would-be contenders with a classic Catch-22, impossible-to-win situation. Not only is the CPD corporate owned, but all five polls are commissioned by the corporate-owned print and television media, which require third-party contenders to appear in the polls before they cover their campaigns. Yet to appeal to voters, candidates need media coverage. Voters will not support third-party candidates without the necessary information on their platforms. Meanwhile, third-party contenders are mentioned

---

184 "Fixing the Presidential Debates," *New York Times*, September 18, 1996.

only in relation to their "spoiler" role in the election. The media bombard us with the message that third-party candidates have no chance of winning, so why jeopardize a Democrat or Republican chance of winning by "wasting your vote?"

Yet another example of the CPD exerting undue powers on our democratic process occurred during the nationally televised debate between Democratic Vice President Al Gore and Republican Governor George W. Bush. Prior to the event, an official from the CPD, accompanied by several police officers, blocked Green Party candidate Ralph Nader from entering the auditorium at the University of Massachusetts as a spectator. "I was excluded on political grounds and no other considerations were communicated," Nader told reporters. "This is the kind of creeping tyranny that has turned away so many voters from the electoral process."[185] It was later revealed that a university student had sent Nader his own ticket to the event.

It would be premature to conclude that American voters do not want more choices in the political process, or that third-party candidates don't stand a chance of winning. In an August 2000 Fox News survey, 64 percent of those polled supported a four-way debate that included Nader and Reform Party candidate Pat Buchanan. Of course, that did not happen. Meanwhile, instead of spending their time reaching out to potential supporters, people like Nader and Buchanan, who offer truly fresh ideas that appeal to millions of Americans, spend much of their time and money in court fighting for the right to participate in the US political process.

Consider the case of Ron Paul, the twelve-term congressman from Texas and a three-time candidate for the presidency, who was visible only due to his invisibility during the Republican 2012 presidential nomination process. The corporate-owned mainstream media made the collective decision to blank the veteran US politician, even though Paul came in second place in the Ames Straw Poll (August 13, 2011), an event that helps to gauge public

---

185   Barry Grey, "US Green Party Candidate Ralph Nader Barred from Site of Presidential Debate," World Socialist website, October 5, 2000.

support for the platforms of the candidates. Paul pulled a hefty 4,671 votes, which was just 152 votes fewer than Michele Bachmann, who came in first place. The next day, however, Paul was conspicuously absent from the talk show circuit and news shows, while candidates like Rick Santorum and John Huntsman, who came in last with sixty-nine votes, received more commentary. Not a single television commentator dared mention the elephant in the room.

The day after Paul's stunning showing, NBC's *Meet the Press* show disgracefully announced: "We have a top tier. It is Mitt Romney, Rick Perry, and Michele Bachmann." That same day, and following the very same script, CBS's *Face the Nation* preferred to hoodwink the nation: "We've got a new top tier, and it's Perry, Mitt Romney, and Bachmann." On August 15, Fox News continued with the "top tier" analogy. "We've got a top tier in this race, at least for now, of Romney, Perry, and Bachmann." [186]

Ron Paul, who wrote the unexpected bestselling book, *End the Fed*, understands the bitter reality of US politics better than anybody. Here he explains, in his calm and congenial manner, why the mainstream media glaringly ignored not only his candidacy for the presidency, but his millions of American supporters: "I am gaining recognition in the campaign, and it's a threat to a lot of people. It's a threat to the military-industrial complex; it's a threat to the bankers, the big corporations who get all the benefit. It's a threat to the people who preach that we have to be…in all these countries (militarily). So I think it's big banks, big money, big corporations and the people who want to be the warmongers. If our views keep growing like they are, it's a real threat to the establishment, so the establishment is well protected by many of the individuals who control the five major networks." [187]

Increasingly, Americans are forced to rely on foreign media sources to get the real story: As RT (Russia Today) explained: "While other candidates have waged for increased military spending and weakening the Constitution to crush the civil liberties of

---

186 "Media Ignoring Ron Paul—Jon Stewart notices," YouTube video, www.youtube.com/watch?v=hF8fPDQmAre.
187 "Media Ignoring Ron Paul," YouTube.

Americans, Paul is trying to take the US out of foreign wars and reinstall freedom for every citizen. As America continues to be ripped by wars and the Pentagon is haemorrhaging money for the sake of executing civilians, Paul's soft-spoken but solid ideas are finding an audience sick with the establishment."[188]

When given a chance to vote for a political alternative to the Democrat-Republican duopoly, Americans respond with enthusiasm. Yet the opportunity never avails itself because the entire US election process has become a corporate-owned sweepstakes with less credibility than a beauty pageant. The mainstream news decides what candidates can and cannot receive media coverage, which of course means that they are deciding the field of candidates that the American people may choose from. This immediately obliterates any hopes for a refreshing wind of change blowing through Washington; it means business as usual for US politicians and their deep-pocket friends from corporate America. Removing corporate influence from the election process is the crucial first step to cleaning up the American political system.[189] Yet that certainly won't be happening any time soon.

Welcome to Koch Industries

With no loss of irony, Charles and David Koch (pronounced "Coke"), the owners of Koch Industries Inc.,[190] are spending obscene amounts of cash to make sure that "big government" does not interfere in your life. Yet the Koch brothers have no problem promoting an anti-democratic agenda that will have no small impact on your life. Armed with a veritable army of well-financed organizations and lobbyists, the Kochs are hauling their damaged product to Capitol Hill, where money talks louder than anywhere

---

188 "Ron Paul Wins Despite Mainstream Smear," Russia Today (RT), December 23, 2011.
189 The 2012 presidential debates were sponsored by Anheuser-Busch, the Howard G. Buffett Foundation, Sheldon S. Cohen, Esq., Crowell & Moring LLP, International Bottled Water Association, the Kovler Fund, Philips, Southwest Airlines, and the YWCA. Source: www.debates.org.
190 Koch Industries, which operates in forty-five US states, is involved in industries as diverse oil and ranching, chemicals and forestry, and consumer products and gas. Koch Industries owns Brawny paper towels, Dixie cups, Stainmaster carpet, Georgia-Pacific lumber, and other popular brand names. Forbes ranks it as the second-largest private company in the nation.

else on the planet. According to a report by the Center for American Progress, Koch nonprofit organizations have contributed "at least $85.9 million to more than 85 different right-wing organizations over the past decade and a half."[191] Meanwhile, the Koch-supported conservative advocacy group, Americans for Prosperity, "spent roughly $45 million for the midterm elections" in 2010, helping to make it the most expensive election in US history. Of that amount, $4.1 million was spent on campaign ads that called for an end to "wasteful federal spending." The glaring irony of that statement, of course, is that much of the "wasteful federal spending" went to bail out Koch's banking and corporate cronies who were responsible for driving the global economy to the abyss due to rigged mortgage schemes and imploding pensions that destroyed millions of middle-class families. But of course, that is not the way Charles and David view their ideological philanthropy. These billionaires would rather focus their attack on "wasteful" government spending that involves health, education, and other social programs that assist millions of needy Americans.

Despite, or because of, the financial collapse of 2008, the Kochs of the world are going on the offensive, making sure that the "pendulum of history" does not complete its cycle and allow for a more progressive, people-oriented political platform. The Koch brothers want to end government regulatory oversight so corporations may act with total impunity; in other words, people like Charles and David Koch have no vested interest in democratic procedure per se. Indeed, the individuals at the top of the corporate hierarchy have a vested interest in democracy only when the subject involves how to suppress it or manage it. "Democratic ideas are most likely to take root among discontented and oppressed classes," observed Richard Hofstadter, "...but they do not appeal to a privileged class that is still amplifying its privileges."[192]

Although the Koch philosophy preaches independence, the message is dripping in hypocrisy. After all, these billionaire broth-

---

191 Tony Carrk, "The Koch Brothers, What You Need to Know About the Financiers of the Radical Right," Center for American Progress, April 2011.
192 Richard Hofstadter, *The American Political Tradition* (New York: Vintage Books Edition, 1989), 7.

ers owe their good fortune in life to a generous inheritance from their father, the late Fred Koch. Thus, the Kochs never ask why it should matter if a person's primary benefactor happens to be the government or a close relative, because the answer is an uncomfortable one: In both cases the beneficiary received a "monetary handout" that he or she did absolutely nothing to earn (actually, the only thing required from inheritors of great wealth is to be born; something they did nothing to contribute to, unlike the government).

Hypocrisy notwithstanding, Charles and David Koch are on a crusade to eliminate "government control" in our lives in the belief that filling the void with corporate power is somehow the answer. (The main difference between government power and corporate power is that at least there is a semblance of control of our government officials courtesy of the ballot box; corporate power has no such internal mechanism to restrain its behavior.) Like many other members of the economic elite, the Kochs refuse to see that all contests—and especially contests of an economic nature, where greed is an ever-present factor—require the supervisory powers of a referee or mediator. For them, the situation is a matter of black and white: The winners and the losers in life both got exactly what they deserved. Despite the flawed philosophy of these individuals, they both continue to play a significant role in rewriting the economic and political rules of the game, which work to reinforce America's move toward tyranny.

Aside from the right-wing Tea Party movement as a whole, the most notorious beneficiary of the Koch blitzkrieg to date is Scott Walker, the Republican governor of Wisconsin. Walker attracted headlines in early 2011 for his attempt to end collective bargaining rights on the part of public-employee unions. The move sparked protests in twenty-seven states as other politicians, including Governor Mitch Daniels of Indiana and John Kasich of Ohio, attempted to impose similar restrictions on public employees. By throwing their financial weight behind such candidates, the Koch brothers believe they are promoting the cause of "freedom and liberty," which applies, of course, only to the corporations and the handful of people who control them. Koch-backed politicians like Walker deregulate to the bone and give corporations the green light to ignore environmental standards, ship jobs overseas, and weaken the already devastated labor unions, in addition to other such "free market" activities. Such an agenda has one goal in mind: the greatest amount of profit for the fewest number of people, and the American middle class certainly does not figure into the calculations.

Meanwhile, the story of the "Kochtopus" gets more entangled as it grows. Not only have the Kochs funded the politicians who are destroying the lives of average Americans, they are helping to pass the very legislation that makes this jolly little nightmare possible. And in order to do that, it is necessary to get chummy with members of the Supreme Court, the very people whom nobody should be getting chummy with. So guess who got an invitation to attend the Koch annual conference, which is dedicated, according to a letter written by Charles Koch himself, "to review strategies for combating the multitude of public policies that threaten to destroy America as we know it"? It seems that the promise of very good food plus accommodations was just too much of a temptation for Antonin Scalia and Clarence Thomas, right-leaning Supreme Court justices who have appeared on several occasions at the Koch brothers' "retreats." Naturally, this created a bit of a stir among those paying attention, especially since Thomas's and Scalia's attendance came shortly before passage of the hugely controversial Citizens United ruling, which, as already discussed, allows domestic and foreign corporations to engage in direct political spending in US elections without public disclosure.

Common Cause, an advocacy group, questioned Justice Thomas's financial disclosure report for 2008, in which he reported that the Federalist Society, an influential conservative legal group, had reimbursed him an undisclosed amount for four days of "transportation, meals and accommodations" at a political retreat in Palm Springs, California, that was organized by the Koch brothers. According to the *New York Times* story, "Common Cause maintains that Justice Thomas should have disqualified himself from last year's landmark campaign finance ruling in the Citizens United case, partly because of his ties to the Koch brothers." [193]

The very fact that the corporate elite must go to such extremes to advance their agenda proves from the start the unpopularity of their activities. If their programs were inherently harmless, why the need for such expensive, conflict-of-interest measures to advance their agenda? Perhaps a better question is why the American people permit these individuals to use the money that consumers—of all political stripes—spend on Koch products to advance a predominantly anti-democratic philosophy? Wouldn't the people eventually abandon a company and its products if they knew that it was funding a political program diametrical to their own personal belief system? That is precisely why blatantly pro-business legislation, like the treacherous Citizens United ruling, is being rammed through with the help of corporate money and political lackeys. Corporations, as well as the politicians, can now hide their shameful identities from the public domain while the destruction of democracy continues unopposed.

ALL THE PRESIDENT'S BUSINESSMEN

Whereas the Koch brothers' manipulation of the political process betrays the corporate interests now dominating America's political system, the rise of a few powerful political families reveals the dynastic tendencies that are the result of that usurpation. Although there is a temptation to refer to the rise of powerful families, such as the Kennedys, Clintons, and the Bushes for example, as some sort of neo-aristocratic "Camelot" movement, that would bestow on these individuals far more dignity and honor than they deserve. It also has the effect of making it seem that their rise to power was preordained by birth and blood—an idea that is wholly repugnant to most Americans, and not least of all to our founders. The truth of the matter is unnerving: The rise of a few

---

193 Eric Lichtblau, "Common Cause Asks Court about Thomas Speech," *New York Times,* February 14, 2011.

powerful, tightly knit individuals and families is symptomatic of corporate-style tyranny, which some commentators have gone so far as to label as neo-fascism.

Today in America, a handful of powerful corporate forces are exerting pressure on the political system to such a degree that to speak of democracy is to sound like a fool and a simpleton. The number of families and individuals who control our political process has dramatically shrunk in direct proportion to the fantastic growth of corporate power. This usurpation of power also explains why the United States gives disproportionate attention to just two political parties, the Democrats and the Republicans: Any serious third-party "faction" would dilute the stranglehold that the corporate world enjoys over our "elected" officials.

In an effort to understand the corporate forces that are now guiding American politics, we must consider some of the individuals who served in the presidential administration of George W. Bush, whose presidency will forever be stained by the so-called War on Terror. Between 2000 and 2008, the American people endured a foreign neoconservative regime that thrived on creating an atmosphere of confusion, fear, and deception among the people. After manipulating the fear factor for eight long years, George W. Bush was replaced by Barack Obama. The change, however, has proved to be merely cosmetic; America—from airports to the workplace—continues to live in the shadow of anxious helplessness. Although much has already been written on the Patriot Act and America's grievous loss of civil liberties, much less has been said about the handful of individuals and corporations that not only profited from this reign of fear, but also pressed for legislation that made war altogether unavoidable.

Although few people questioned the neoconservative push for war against the Taliban in Afghanistan following the terrorist attacks of September 11, 2001, the same cannot be said for the bloodthirsty military adventure that followed. This marked the moment when the United States, the victim of one of the most dramatic terror attacks in recent history, managed to quickly forfeit much of the international outpouring of sympathy and condolences it had received in the months following 9/11. What was it that caused people from all nationalities, including some of our most ardent allies, to voice their opposition to American behavior? The reason for the global change of heart is that the Bush administration inexplicably went on the warpath against Iraq, a sovereign nation that had no connection to the events of 9/11. Despite the fact the UN weapons inspectors were on the ground in the Arab republic searching for weapons of mass destruction (none were ever found then or later), the Bush administration ignored their work, launching a unilateral assault against the sovereign government of Saddam Hussein on March 19, 2003. Then the corporate gravy train really started to pour.

THE CARLYLE GROUP

One of the biggest benefactors of the war in Iraq was a private equity firm that invests in heavily regulated government industries, specifically telecommunications and defense. Although many companies sell their products to the US government, the Carlyle Group is in a class by itself with an A-list of former heads of state that includes former President George H. W. Bush, former Secretary of State James Baker, former UK Prime Minister John Major, and former National Security Director Frank Carlucci. Last but not least, among the company's investors were members of the family of Osama bin Laden. Some might call that a conflict of interest, especially where the interest of American security is concerned.

As late as March 2001, just six months before the terror attacks of 9/11, it was reported that George H. W. Bush, the father of then-President George W. Bush, was cavorting with Saudi officials and royalty with the sole purpose of attracting investments. "In getting business for Carlyle, Mr. Bush has been impressive," wrote the *New York Times*. "His meeting with the crown prince was followed by a yacht cruise and private dinners with Saudi officials, including King Fahd, all on behalf of Carlyle, which has extensive interests in the Middle East."[194]

---

194 Leslie Wayne, "Elder Bush in Big G.O.P. Cast Toiling for Top Equity Firm," *New York Times*, March 5, 2001.

How is it possible that the president's father, himself a former president, not to mention a former CIA director with the deepest connections, could continue doing business with the Saudis given that the terrorist trail led directly to Osama bin Laden's cave? After all, it's not as if the US intelligence community was oblivious to the threat posed by al-Qaeda. Indeed, in the weeks and months before 9/11, FBI field offices were sounding alarms about an increase of activity among suspected terrorists residing inside the country. The Bush administration chose to ignore them. Then, on August 6, 2001, one month before the terror attacks that would change the world, a presidential daily briefing with the screaming title "Bin Laden Determined to Strike Inside of the United States" landed on the president's desk. Still, the Bush administration took no additional measures to counter the warnings. Nor did Bush's father seem overly concerned about his Carlyle connections.

When 9/11 blew up in Washington's lap, the Carlyle Group, which was holding its annual meeting on the very morning of the attacks in New York City (a member of the bin Laden clan was also in attendance), was suddenly put in a very uncomfortable situation. Before any sort of official investigation had begun, the American news channels were screaming in one corporate-owned voice that the mastermind behind the attacks was none other than Osama bin Laden. It was later determined that fifteen of the nineteen men said to have commandeered the four airplanes hailed from Saudi Arabia. Whatever discomforts the Carlyle Group may have experienced when its shady business dealings with the bin Laden clan was exposed came to nothing. That's because all members of the bin Laden family living in the United States at the time of the attacks were whisked out of the country—aboard commercial jets, no less—soon after the suicidal hijackings that left three thousand Americans dead. As reported in the 9/11 commission draft report, "After the airspace reopened, six chartered flights with 142 people, mostly Saudi Arabian nationals, departed from the United States between Sept. 14 and 24. One flight, the so-called bin Laden flight, departed the United States on September 20 with 26 passengers, most of them relatives of Osama bin Laden."[195] It's tempting to question if those frequent fliers got courtesy drinks compliments of the Carlyle Group on their one-way flight out of Dodge.

The one thing we know the bin Laden family did not receive was a good old-fashioned detective grilling of the sort we've all seen a million times before in the movies. The relatives of Osama bin Laden were never formally questioned by a single American intelligence officer before exiting the country. Naturally, it took the work of a foreign reporter to pose the uncomfortable questions that his American colleagues just could not articulate. Greg Palast, a political commentator for BBC Television's *Newsnight*, risked the question: "What made this new president [George W. Bush] take particular care to protect the Saudis, even to the point of stymieing his own intelligence agencies? The answer kept coming back to the Bush family's connection with Carlyle. That connection influenced a policy that ordered our intelligence agencies to say, 'Hands off the Saudis.'"[196] Later, the Bush administration demanded extensive deletions in a House and Senate Intelligence Committee report on 9/11, especially in the section that dealt with the role played by Saudi Arabia and other foreign governments.

Despite the fact that Carlyle had relatives of international terrorists among its investors, this did not stop it from cashing in big on the War on Terror. One of its subsidiary companies, United Defense, had been lobbying to sell the Pentagon its Crusader Advanced Field Artillery System, an unwieldy and expensive weapons systems that critics said clashed with the US Army's new lean and mean look. All that changed, however, with the terrorist attacks on New York and Washington, and a bit of help from the Bush father-son tandem. On December 13, 2001, one day before Carlyle announced that it would take United Defense public on the New York Stock Exchange, President Bush signed off on a defense appropriation bill that included $487.3 million for the Crusader system. The next day, Carlyle earned a cool $237 million

---

195 "National Commission on Terrorist Attacks upon the United States, Threats and Responses in 2001, Staff Statement No. 10, The Saudi Flights," 12.
196 Greg Palast, "See No Evil," *TomPaine.com*, March 1, 2003.

selling very hot United shares on Wall Street. Not a bad day for the Carlyle Group; not a bad day for the Bush family.

Carlyle denies that it lobbies the federal government, which is probably true since the company is already a de facto arm of the federal government. After all, how much lobbying would the father of the president really need to do on behalf of a company where the former is gainfully employed? "It should be a deep cause for concern that a closely held company like Carlyle can simultaneously have directors and advisers that are doing business and making money and also advising the president of the United States," said Peter Eisner, managing director of the Center for Public Integrity, a non-profit public watchdog. "The problem comes when private business and public policy blend together."[197] The problem with Carlyle, however, was more than just the obvious conflict of interest between members of the Bush family, one who just happened to be the president.

In February 2001, just months before the attacks of 9/11, Carlyle Board Chairman Frank Carlucci and Vice President Dick Cheney met with Defense Secretary Donald Rumsfeld at the same time that the Carlyle Group had several multibillion-dollar projects under consideration (Carlucci and Rumsfeld are old college classmates, while the political careers of Cheney and Rumsfeld began way back in the Ford administration). There remains the nagging question as to what motivated Carlucci, a former deputy director of the CIA who joined Carlyle in 1989, to invest heavily into the defense industry at a time when other businessmen with more investing experience were shunning the sector. Was he privy to some inside information on future events that made a small group of investors very wealthy? Speaking on the subject of Carlucci's friendship with Donald Rumsfeld, Carlyle spokesman Chris Ullman said: "I assure you he doesn't lobby. That's the last thing he'd do. You'd have to know Carlucci to know he'd never do that, and you'd have to know Rumsfeld to know it wouldn't matter."[198] Since

197 Oliver Burkeman and Julian Borger, "The Ex-Presidents' Club," *Guardian*, October 31, 2001.
198 Mark Fineman, "Arms Buildup Is a Boon to Firm Run by Big Guns," *Los Angeles Times*, January 10, 2002.

most Americans are not buddies with either Carlucci or Rumsfeld, we have to take Ullman's esteemed opinion of the two men.

However, even if we are wrong and there was no illicit exchange of inside secrets, the public should not be forced to entertain such "conspiracy theories" in the first place. The problem with this sort of crony collaboration, meanwhile, goes beyond the banal desire to make a quick buck. There exists the very real danger, or perhaps *temptation* is the better word, to lead the nation into a war where thousands of innocents will be injured or killed, as was clearly the case in the illegitimate war in Iraq. After all, Carlyle certainly understood it was in the position to turn a massive profit in the event of war, which makes the military invasion of Iraq look all the more sinister.

Whatever the case may be, it is impossible not to draw ugly conclusions from the available information. Carlyle was doing business with family members of the world's preeminent terrorist who somehow managed to evade America's multibillion-dollar defense system with nineteen wily Arabs armed with nothing more than box cutters and brass balls. Yet, even as the crime scene was still smoldering over Manhattan and the Pentagon, the Bush people grant the bin Laden clan permission to exit the country without making them sit through a single interrogation session. After all, we know how much the US government hates to inconvenience people at airports. Later, the Bush administration invaded Iraq despite the fact that the country had no connection to al-Qaeda and 9/11. The question is elementary detective work: Was the decision to go to war against Iraq made on the supposed threat posed by Saddam Hussein's regime, or on the basis of the war profits that stood to be gained in the event of a conflict? What was guiding American foreign policy? Rational, strategic planning on the part of the military, or shareholder meetings inside of closed-door corporate boardrooms? Who stood to gain the most from war with Iraq? Certainly not the American people and certainly not the Iraqis.

As the *Guardian* put it: "Carlyle has become the thread which indirectly links American military policy...to the personal financial fortunes of its celebrity employees, not least of all the president's father."[199] Indeed, it is no secret that Bush the Younger harbored a personal vendetta against the late Iraqi leader, Saddam Hussein, "the guy who tried to kill my dad." Taken together—the free pass to go after your father's sworn enemy, as well as the chance to make a lot of money in the process—may be simply too much of a temptation for a "war president" to refuse. In the final analysis, the Carlyle Group certainly played a role in the decision to go to war against Iraq, and this fact underscores the need to remove corporate lobbyists from the halls of power in Washington once and for all.

HELLO, HALLIBURTON

Nobody will ever accuse Dick Cheney, the former US vice president under George W. Bush, of not recognizing a golden business opportunity when he sees one. Shortly after former President George H. W. Bush had declared an end to military operations in the first Gulf War (August 1990–February 1991), Cheney, then serving as the Pentagon chief, paid a Halliburton subsidiary called Brown & Root $9 million to examine how private military companies (PMCs) could provide support for US soldiers during times of war. Apparently, Cheney was not disappointed by the results of the study because he went on to become the CEO of Halliburton in 1995.

During Cheney's control of Halliburton, the company occasionally behaved as if it were above the law. "The United States had concluded that Iraq, Libya, and Iran supported terrorism and had imposed strict sanctions on them," reported *Mother Jones,* an independent news organization. "Yet during Cheney's tenure at Halliburton the company did business in all three countries. In the case of Iraq, Halliburton legally evaded U.S. sanctions by conducting its oil-service business through foreign subsidiaries."[200]

---

199 Burkeman and Borger, "The Ex-Presidents' Club."
200 Conor Friedersdorf, "Remembering Why Americans Loathe Dick Cheney," *Mother Jones,* August 30, 2011.

Halliburton was also accused of overcharging the US government on various projects.

These minor flaws of judgement, however, did not prevent George W. Bush from choosing Cheney to be his running mate in the 2000 elections. In fact, Cheney's willingness to bend the rules probably only served to enhance his credentials. Not surprisingly, when Cheney became vice president the tendency for unscrupulous behavior continued. In December 2001, Kellogg, Brown and Root (KBR), the subsidiary of Cheney's former company, secured a ten-year contract from the Pentagon to rebuild Iraq's oil industry and other services. It should be noted that KBR "won" the deal without any second-party competitive bidding. Meanwhile, Cheney, in addition to owning thousands of stock shares, was still pulling a hefty deferred salary from Halliburton.

In 2003, the same year that the US military launched a "preemptive strike" against Iraq, Cheney had drawn a cool $173,437 from his former company. The fair and obvious question is: Was the decision to attack Iraq based upon the profits to be gained in rebuilding the country after it had been destroyed? According to one estimate, Halliburton KBR has been "awarded at least $2.5 billion to construct and run military bases, some in secret locations, as part of the Army's Logistics Civil Augmentation Program (LOGCAP)."[201] So while Cheney had been viewed in some quarters as America's "shadow president," who "treated the State Department and the National Security Council as foreign enemies,"[202] he now had a de facto shadow military to complete his junta.

This leads us to what ranks as one of the darkest chapters in American history. KBR was also responsible for overhauling the forty-five-square-mile slice of Cuban hell known as the Guantanamo Bay Detention Camp (GTMO). After the US Justice Department supported the Bush administration's claims that the "illegal combatants" in GTMO were beyond the reach of the US legal system, the fun and games really began in the "War on Terror." The

---

201 Barry Yeoman, "Soldiers of Good Fortune," *Mother Jones*, May/June 2003.
202 Jacob Heilbrunn, "The Shadow President," *New York Times*, October 12, 2008.

first twenty detainees arrived on January 11, 2002, and although the United States has held prisoners of war in the past, the way these detainees were treated in GTMO said far more about the captors than the captives.

Shorn of their most basic human rights, including legal representation, the detainees were brought to the pleasure island handcuffed and forced to kneel inside barbed-wire enclosures with military personnel right at their side. But the brutal, sadistic treatment did not end there. The detainees were forced to wear heavy gloves, face masks, goggles, and earmuffs—something euphemistically called sensory deprivation—in the oppressive Cuban heat. It should be mentioned that Guantanamo Bay is probably the best naturally fortified prison in the world. As a rugged military outpost surrounded by steep hills to the north and shark-infested waters to the south, escaping from GTMO is highly unlikely. The question remains why this facility, over which Cheney and Halliburton had no small sway, found it necessary to behave more like animals than the alleged terrorists they were holding? Why was it necessary to make the detainees lose their minds? Was it to limit their mental ability to defend themselves in a civil court of law (a day that will never come; all remaining detainees will be tried by secret military tribunal)?

The outrageous abuse of human rights prevalent inside GTMO was not limited to that rocky American outpost. Like a cancer that spreads quickly throughout the body, the human rights abuses at this Cuban outpost infected a number of European countries. In a report released by a European Parliament special committee, eleven EU nations were accused of cooperating with the United States in the so-called "extraordinary rendition" of detainees in the Bush administration's War on Terror.[203] Of the dozen or so countries that cooperated in one way or another with the US intelligence services, one of the governments has made an effort to come clean. Polish President Donald Tusk, coming just short of

---

203 "Europe Knew about Secret CIA Flights," *Spiegel Online*, November 11, 2006. The EU parliamentary report claims that "1,245 flights operated by the CIA have flown into European airspace, or stopped over at European airports." It also mentions evidence of a CIA secret prison in Poland.

blurting out the filthy truth, admitted in early 2012 that Poland had become the "political victim" of American foreign policy.

"Poland will no longer be a country where politicians—even if they are working arm in arm with the world's greatest super-power—could make some deal somewhere under the table and then it would never see daylight," said Tusk, who entered office four years after the American black site was shuttered. "Poland is a democracy where national and international law must be observed." There is little doubt as to whom the Polish president was speaking about. His comments came just days after Poland's former intelligence minister, Zbigniew Siemiatowski, was charged for his role in letting the Americans commit what amounts to serious crimes against humanity on the territory of Poland.[204]

Again, the same question arises as to what was the motivation behind such egregious behavior. In order to justify the need for an illegal prison beyond US legal jurisdiction, as well as justify at the same time the massive subsidies to keep Halliburton's government checks coming, it was necessary to fill Guantanamo Bay with prisoners. Thus, it should come as no surprise that many of the detainees at GTMO are innocent of the charges being leveled against them. Yet, despite President Barack Obama's campaign pledge to shutter the barbaric facility, it remains open to this day. This is due in no small part to the work of, yes, former Vice President Dick Cheney, who, in retirement and despite basement-level ratings in public opinion polls, appeared on news stations warning against giving the GTMO detainees civil trials on US territory. Cheney thinks that nothing less than military tribunals for the two hundred detainees would suffice.

This brings up another question: Why was the Bush administration in general and Dick Cheney in particular so adamantly opposed to giving the detainees a fair and transparent civil trial in the United States? After all, even the Nazis, as ruthless and inhumane as they were, received an internationally monitored hearing

204 Vanessa Gera, "CIA Secret Prisons: Polish Leaders Break Silence about Black Site," Associated Press.

at the Nuremburg Trials on the territory of Germany. Although the United States dragged up to eleven European nations into its "extraordinary rendition" plot, the US authorities are showing no desire to allow foreign representatives to supervise the military tribunals. For all intents and purposes, the GTMO detainees remain in a black site on a dark corner of Cuba where all of their human rights have been obliterated.

NAKED BODY SCANNERS, ANYONE?

Yet another American political adviser whose business pursuits presented a conflict of interest is Michael Chertoff, who served as the secretary of homeland security from February 15, 2005, until January 21, 2009. This leadership role gave him exclusive control over a whole phalanx of security departments, including the Transportation Security Administration (TSA). In the words of one critic, Michael Chertoff "sits at the heart of the giant security nexus created in the wake of 9/11, in effect creating a shadow homeland security agency."[205] Thus, the uncomfortable question arises: *Quis custodiet ipsos custodies?* (Who will guard us from the guardians?) Just days after President Barack Obama was sworn into office in January 2009, Chertoff launched the Chertoff Group. He brought with him to his firm about a dozen top officials from the Department of Homeland Security, as well as CIA director General Michael Hayden and other top brass.

Less than a year later, enter Umar Farouk Abdulmutallab, who allegedly attempted to ignite an explosive device hidden inside his underwear on Northwest Flight 253. Chertoff was immediately ubiquitous on the news channels, calling for the federal government to purchase full-body scanners for all airports. Despite the many lingering doubts about the system, including invasion of privacy concerns (the technology has been described as a "virtual strip search" by privacy advocates) and the radiation that the machines

---

205 Marcus Baram, "Fear Pays: Chertoff, Ex-Security Officials Slammed for Cashing in on Government Experience," *Huffington Post*, November 23, 2010.

emit, Chertoff called for the end of restrictive legislation that would regulate how, where, when, and why US passengers would be forced to submit to such humiliation. "Congress should…fund a large-scale deployment of next-generation systems," [206] Chertoff wrote in an op-ed piece one week after the mysterious Christmas Day event. The handwringing on behalf of the former head of Homeland Security prompted the government to immediately purchase three hundred additional full-body scanners. Questions concerning privacy issues and exposing frequent fliers to radiation from the machines are played down. Chertoff has said the machines expose the body to "more radiation than is experienced in daily life."[207] Then he called on the current administration to "stand firm against privacy ideologues, for whom every security measure is unacceptable."

What the former secretary of homeland security failed to inform the public, however, is that his company represents Rapiscan, the company that manufactures the very machines that Chertoff wants the government to spend billions of dollars on (Chertoff disclosed the relationship that he has with manufacturers of the technology only on a CNN program, and only when challenged on the issue by the host). How convenient that the former homeland secretary chief would become the official spokesperson for airport scanners, the very system that would make him a very wealthy man if installed nationwide.

More than one rights group called into question Chertoff's use of his former government credentials to promote a product that benefits his clients. "Mr. Chertoff should not be allowed to abuse the trust the public has placed in him as a former public servant to privately gain from the sale of full-body scanners under the pretense that the scanners would have detected this type of explosive," said Kate Hanni, founder of FlyersRights.org, which opposes the use of body scanners in airports.[208] In a separate interview, Hanni said that "Chertoff…is basically promoting his clients

---

206 Michael Chertoff, "Former Homeland Security Chief Argues for Whole-Body Imaging," *Washington Post*, January 1, 2010.
207 Chertoff, *Washington Post*, January 1, 2010.
208 "Group Slams Chertoff on Scanner Promotion," *Boston Globe*, January 5, 2010.

and exploiting that fear to make money. Fear is a commodity, and they are selling it."[209]

There is just one last twist to this tale that can almost be described as insider trading. In August 2012, a federal appeals court ordered the TSA to explain why it hasn't complied with the court's order to conduct public hearings involving the rules pertaining to the whole-body imaging scanners installed at US airport security zones.

According to an article in *Wired,* the TSA breached federal law when it introduced the technology into US airports. "The three-judge appellate court, which is one stop from the Supreme Court, said that the Transportation Security Administration breached federal law in 2009 when it formally adopted the Advanced Imaging Technology scanners as the 'primary' method of screening. The judges—while allowing the scanners to be used—said the TSA violated the Administrative Procedures Act for failing to have a 90-day public comment period, and ordered the agency to undertake one."[210] As of this writing, that order remains unfulfilled, while American citizens—from children to grandmothers—are still being harassed at the border by TSA guards.

WHAT IS TO BE DONE?

First, it must be stressed that nothing was illegal about the behavior of the individuals and their affiliated companies described above. In fact, many would argue they used their public positions and business prowess to safeguard America. At any rate, however, such behavior is open to speculation and forces the public to entertain all sorts of "conspiracy theories" about their leaders, which only serves to fortify our distrust of government. It is no secret that politicians, generally speaking, represent some of the least trusted people on the planet; we should not give them the opportunity to further tarnish their already stained image.

209 Baram, "Fear Pays."
210 David Kravets, "Court Demands TSA Explain Why It Is Defying Nude Body Scanner Order," *Wired,* August 1, 2012.

Removing corporate power from the political equation will go far in simplifying matters, as well as introducing some light and transparency into the democratic process where now stand brick walls and closed doors.

This will be no easy task. As evident by the activities of the Koch brothers and their vast network of advocacy groups they fund, and the control over the US election process, those at the top of the corporate-political pyramid are attempting to defy the very laws of "political nature" by seizing the pendulum when it is on their side, preventing it from performing the next stage of its continuous cycle. According to the rule of history, which, as we have described, swings between conservative and liberal tendencies, America should be passing through a period of progressivism at this very moment. Yet, thanks to the concerted efforts of the corporate elite, in collaboration with their political servants, not to mention a supine Supreme Court, the social and political evolution of the American people has been stunted, halted in its tracks. Yet efforts to block a civic-minded political awakening cannot last indefinitely. They may be able to delay the process, but this only causes the human machinery to overheat until some sort of potentially cataclysmic backlash occurs. Unless a more progressive political program is allowed to grow, a total breakdown of the social machinery is inevitable.

As inhabitants of a democracy, it is our civic duty to eject corporate power from our political system. Actually, it is more than a duty; it is a foregone conclusion, *fait accompli*. And that is because there is no escaping from corporate tyranny in these hyperconnected days. In a different day and age, we could load up the wagon and shotgun, like our European ancestors, and seek out a new land when the oppression at home becomes intolerable. Today, escaping to some enchanted frontier is no longer an option. The "American frontier" has been incorporated, privatized, and fenced in one way or another, while, at the same time, the majority of people are dependent upon corporate benefaction for their daily bread and butter. "The single separate citizen has no longer the power and independence that he had," lamented Bertrand Russell. "Our age is one of organization, and its conflicts are between organizations, not between separate individuals."[211]

Given the rumblings of economic and political discontent (which the terrorist attacks of 9/11 managed to temporarily check), the American people fully comprehend their plight with regards to corporate power. "The game is…up," author and journalist Chris Hedges has written. "The clock is ticking toward internal and external collapse. Even our corporate overlords no longer believe the words they utter. They rely instead on the security and surveillance state for control. The rumble of dissent that rises from the Occupy Movements terrifies them. It creates a new narrative. It exposes their exploitation and cruelty. And it shatters the absurdity of their belief system."[212]

It needs repeated: Corporate power must be restrained from playing games inside the political system. Democracy is too fragile and limited a franchise to permit such a disruptive presence. After all, even in matters related to warfare, it is generally acknowledged that this is too serious a business to be left solely to the military establishment. Intelligent thinkers, or at least the state, must step in and control the voracious military complex; otherwise it will shortly control, or destroy, the state through sheer recklessness. This same logic has not been applied equally to the economic sector, however, in the belief that the acumen of the businessmen (outstanding moral beings that they are) will always make the appropriate decisions, or that the "invisible hand" of the marketplace will magically guide society. We fail to understand, however, that the economic sector is every bit as lethal as the military sector in terms of destroying lives; the only difference is that the one kills with a gun, the other with a calculator.

The corporate elite have come to confuse their own success for the success of the people; if the corporate world is doing well, they believe, the nation as a whole must be doing well also. As one writer described the situation: "Those at the top…fail to understand how much their wealth and power is a function of their environment."[213]

---

211 Bertrand Russell, *History of Western Philosophy* (London: Rutledge, 1946), 582.
212 Chris Hedges and Joe Sacco, *Days of Destruction, Days of Revolt* (New York: Nation Books, 2012), XII.
213 Maura Kelly, "Trickle-Down Distress: How America's Broken Meritocracy Drives Our National Anxiety Epidemic," *Atlantic*, July 3, 2012.

So the battle against excessive corporate power must be fought in the political realm. Yet the relationship between the corporate sector and the world of politics is so deep that even introducing the issue of corporate power permeating inside our political system is prohibited. Unfortunately, the American people never fully considered the possibility that their cherished Constitution would be forced to include corporate bodies as de facto individuals. Whether the enemy was concentrated economic forces or tyrannical political authority, the Constitution was designed to protect Americans from arbitrary power regardless of the form. We must close the back door that has been opened in the Constitution, granting extreme economic entities "personhood," which tramples upon our liberty and freedom.

In closing this chapter, I would like to reproduce a warning made at the height of the Great Depression, which forewarns of the excessive powers that the corporate world would come to enjoy at the expense of the state and its citizens: "The rise of the modern corporation has brought a concentration of economic power which can compete on equal terms with the modern state....The state seeks in some aspects to regulate the corporation, while the corporation, steadily becoming more powerful, makes every effort to avoid such regulation. Where its own interests are concerned, it even attempts to dominate the state. The future may see the economic organism, now typified by the corporation, not only on an equal plane with the state, but possibly even superseding it as the dominant form of social organization. The law of corporations, accordingly, might well be considered as a potential constitutional law for the new economic state, while business practice is increasingly assuming the aspect of economic statesmanship."[214]

We need to reflect upon the contradictory nature of democracy in America—existing as it does inside the most ruthless form of capitalism on the planet. When the people are forced to compete against corporate power in order to preserve their basic freedom, liberty, and democratic representation, something has already gone wrong with the system.

---

214 A. A. Berle Jr. and G. C. Means, *The Modern Corporation and Private Property* (New York: Macmillan Company, 1932), 356.

CHAPTER VI
Globalization's Cracked Foundation

"Contrary to the received wisdom, global markets are not unregulated. They are regulated to produce inequality."

— KEVIN WATKINS

In order to truly appreciate the full extent of the damage being inflicted on our local communities, it is necessary to look at the big picture. Since democracy begins and ends with the people, it logically follows that democracy should be most dynamic at the local level. As we push the borders of globalization to the breaking point, however, our democratic institutions are not keeping pace with the dramatic changes. Judging by the behavior of the largest global institutions, such as the International Monetary Fund and World Bank, our present economic, social, and political plight is no accident. It was designed to be a nightmare by a few individuals at the top of the global pyramid. In any case, permitting large-scale conglomerations into our communities by virtue of nothing more than size is an extremely dangerous experiment and one that threatens the very meaning of community and democracy; indeed, the very existence of democracy hangs in the balance.

Due to the inner dynamics of globalization, our political system is capable of turning out only a bunch of cheats, charlatans, and hypocrites, willing to sell out the people to a tightly knit gang of bankers, financial consultants, and CEOs. Any person who aspires to government office must speak the cant of democracy, yet democracy, for all intents and purposes, is a dead word; better to rename what we really have today—"demo-mockery"—than to continue pretending that a single politician is fighting in our corner against corporate power. As Professor John Dunn has observed, "We have all become democrats in theory at just that stage of history at which it has become virtually impossible for us in practice to organize our social life in a democratic fashion any longer."[215]

LOTS OF CAVEATS, LITTLE CHANGE

In 1996, three years before the city of Seattle became the site of the world's first major protests against globalization, the world's movers and shakers were assembling for the annual World Economic Forum (WEF) conference in Davos, Switzerland, as they had been doing peacefully since their first meeting in 1971. This time around, however, an uninvited cloud darkened the ski slopes and meeting rooms of the elite venue, which was betrayed by its theme, "Sustaining Globalization." As the leaders of this forum had correctly foreseen, a groundswell of grassroots hostility against the perceived injustices of globalization was beginning to rise up across the sleepy global village.

Prior to the kickoff of this downbeat Davos meeting, Klaus Schwab and Claude Smadja, the original organizers of the WEF, warned in an opinion piece in the *International Tribune* that the process of economic globalization "has entered a critical phase in which economic and political relationships, both globally and within countries, are being painfully restructured...with height-

---

215 John Dunn, *Western Political Theory in the Face of the Future* (Cambridge University Press, Canto, 1993), 29.

ened mass insecurity resulting in the rise of a new brand of populist politicians."[216]

The authors rightly foresaw that the road to open global markets had entered a dangerous and unpredictable new phase as public discontent was searching for its political voice. Indeed, the opinion was gaining ground that free and open markets, while a major boon for corporations, invariably meant desperation for the majority of the world's inhabitants. Schwab and Smadja went on to admit that the international financial institutions (namely, the IMF, World Trade Organization, and World Bank) were not merely fiddling with the financial policies of states, but were working to change economic and political legislation in order to lay the groundwork for a more business-friendly world. "The globalization process," they wrote, "is in essence a tremendous redistribution of economic power at the world level, which will increasingly translate into a redistribution of political power."[217]

Now that is certainly a mouthful. Clearly, the financial institutions, as the primary functionaries of "the globalization process," were not simply writing massive, high-interest checks for new capitalist ventures together with their gratuitous advice. They were, and still are, working vigorously behind the scenes with our political leaders to amend the social contracts of sovereign states to promote the interests of corporate power. Meanwhile, democratic debate on these highly controversial matters is a privileged pastime for only the economic and political elite. The "redistribution of economic power at the world level," which will "translate into a redistribution of political power," is continuing without the benefit of democratic due process, that is, unless we somehow believe that permitting a handful of financiers to speak for the multitude behind shuttered doors is democracy in action.

---

216   Klaus Schwab and Claude Smadja, "Start Taking the Backlash Against Globalization Seriously," *International Herald Tribune*, February 1, 1996.
217   During the Valdai Conference in Moscow in 2008, of which both Karl Schwab and I were participants, I asked him if his opinions about the global economy had changed since penning the abovementioned article. He responded: "I believe that at this point, with international markets so volatile, that any outcome is possible."

"Globalization tends to de-link the fate of the corporation from the fate of its employees," Schwab and Smadja continued, as they attempted to explain the source of the "popular scepticism" toward globalization. "In the past, higher profits meant more job security and better wages. The way transnational corporations have to operate to compete in the global economy means that it is now routine to have corporations announce new profit increases along with a new wave of layoffs." Yes, it is easy to see how such a strategy would be a hard sell, and judging by the current economic realities, Schwab and Smadja were pretty much on the money in their grim prognosis. Meanwhile, precious few leaders are speaking out on behalf of the people.

"Globalization is a fact of life," Kofi Annan, the former UN secretary-general said in a speech at Davos in 1999. "But I believe we have underestimated its fragility. The problem is this: The spread of markets far outpaces the ability of societies and their political systems to adjust to them, let alone guide the course they take. History teaches us that such an imbalance between the economic, social, and political realms can never be sustained for very long."[218] Annan then challenged the corporate world to enter into a formal "compact" with the United Nations to protect and promote human rights, labor, and environmental practices in the countries where it does business. Until people have confidence in the global economy, he added, it "will be fragile and vulnerable—vulnerable to backlash from all the 'isms' of our post-Cold War world: protectionism, populism, nationalism, ethnic chauvinism, fanaticism, and terrorism." The assembled corporate and political elite politely applauded Annan's initiative, and then quietly returned to their sheltered elitist worlds where the same self-defeating practices continue. Indeed, with every new gathering of the global elite, the perennial handwringing continues.

In August, 2006, seven years after Kofi Annan challenged the business community to meet the people halfway in an effort to make globalization beneficial for everyone, the newly reinstated

---

218 Alan Cromwell, "Davos Warned of Economic Backlash," *New York Times*, February 1, 1999.

Federal Reserve chairman, Ben Bernanke, was issuing yet another caveat, this one over the threat of "social and political opposition" against the new economic realities. "Further progress in global economic integration should not be taken for granted," he told the Federal Reserve's annual symposium at the mountain resort of Jackson Hole, Wyoming. The Fed chairman went on to say that in this period of globalization, "the social and political opposition to openness can be strong," and this is happening "because changes in the patterns of production are likely to threaten the livelihoods of some workers and the profits of some firms, even when these changes lead to greater productivity and output overall."

In other words, the end (global economic integration and corporate profits) justifies the means (worsening labor conditions). The "livelihoods of some workers" takes a backseat to the eternal quest for "greater productivity and output." Considering the regularity of such caveats, it is evident that our economic leaders understand that persistent tampering with social legislation in order to promote corporate interests will eventually spark a political backlash. Thus, they are simply issuing warnings on their own policy, which they understand to be drastically short-sighted and single-minded. The warnings never instigate real change, nor are they intended to. The corporate elite continue to push an internationalist agenda that is becoming increasingly unpopular, and, given the recent global economic downturn, dangerous for everybody.

The economic windfall that globalization and free markets promised to deliver never materialized because our business and political leaders continue to bank on self-serving corporations as opposed to the people. Thus, we are left with a form of corporate-backed "creative destruction" that is only really creative at destroying the workforce.

"Trade policy has put low- and middle-wage workers in the United States in direct competition with typically much lower-wage workers in the rest of the world," the Center for Economic and Policy Research (CEPR) reported. "A dysfunctional immigration system has left a growing share of our immigrant population at the mercy of their employers, while increasing competitive pressures on low-wage workers born in the United States."[219] The study concludes that "these policy decisions, *rooted in politics,* are the main explanations for the decline in the economy's ability to generate good jobs." So much for blaming the Great Recession for all of our woes.

"No one dares admit the degree to which the trade system is actually manipulated," commented Barry Lynn, a senior fellow at the New America Foundation, "not by any state but by companies built to straddle many states. No one dares admit the degree to which these companies tend to destroy not merely soft social infrastructure, such as pensions and wages, but basic production infrastructures."[220] And as usual, it is the middle class that is feeling the brunt of the changes. As the CEPR report revealed: The US economy "has lost about one-third (28 to 38 percent) of its capacity to generate good jobs."

"There was a time ten years ago when it seemed like globalization was consensual, and there were very few remaining questions about whether it was a good thing," Jeffrey Frieden, an expert on global economics at Harvard University, told the Christian Science Monitor in the months preceding the 2007 crash. 'The reality of the situation comes with a caveat: Globalization "can make everyone better off, so long as you compensate for the losers."[221] Such social benevolence, however, does not fit the logic of economic liberalization, a euphemistic term for an economic philosophy that is far more interested in liberalizing the choices for the corporations as opposed to those who have become its desperate dependents—or in some cases, victims.

Since the founders of Davos issued their warning shot across the bow of democracy over a decade ago, the trajectory of globalization has remained true to its iron track and continues to trade downward in its quest for continually cheaper and freely acces-

---

219 Schmitt and Jones, p. 1.
220 Barry Lynn, "Globalization Must Be Saved by the Radical Global Utopians," *Financial Times,* May 30, 2006, 13.
221 Mark Trumbull, "Backlash Grows against Free Trade," *Christian Science Monitor,* February 18, 2007.

sible markets. This state of affairs is symptomatic of a far deeper problem, directly connected to the powers that were sanctioned to the corporate and financial world a long time ago. Today, what the system is severely lacking is democratic reform, not economic reform.

As more details emerge about the reckless behavior that triggered the Great Recession of 2008, the aftershocks of which we are still feeling today, an increasing number of Americans cannot shake the feeling that they have become the victim of a massive economic misadventure. "Men have a sufficient natural instinct for what is true," Aristotle wrote, "and usually do arrive at the truth."[222] What people ultimately decide to do with that unsettling "truth" is another question. However, it is necessary to reflect only upon the cruel lessons of the French Revolution, or Russia's painful seventy-year fling with communism, to understand how far the masses may wander astray in order to achieve a semblance of social equality and justice. It would be a mistake to believe that America is exceptional enough to escape such unfortunate social upheavals.

CLOSED-DOOR DEMOCRACY

Symptomatic of the elite's escapist mentality is their penchant for private gatherings and private meetings, far removed from the inconvenience of democratic procedure; despite our proclaimed attachment to democratic principles, this archaic tradition infects far too many organizations at the very core.[223] Indeed, for members of the corporate elite, there is no greater irritation than to have some group of disgruntled demonstrators protesting outside their window while they, the architects of the new world order, are busy as beavers writing the rules of globalization. So we must ask if the acceptance of liberal, laissez-faire market principles automatically

---

222 Aristotle, *Rhetoric* (New York: Dover Publications, 2004), 5.
223 Following the "Battle of Seattle," the US government developed the concept of so-called "free speech zones" where protesters are permitted to assemble, thus drawing criticism from those who argue that all of the United States should be a "free speech zone," and not just those segregated areas conveniently chosen for their distance from the event.

entails the loss of democratic representation, not to mention economic independence for the great majority of society. Do the workers of the world need a constitution?

There exists no legitimate political or economic tract that suggests it is in the spirit of democracy, or even capitalism, that controversial economic issues should be withheld from public debate. Even the regularly misinterpreted Adam Smith would quickly alienate such an ill-conceived notion. As the father of capitalist theory famously observed in 1776, "People of the same trade seldom meet together, even for merriment or diversion, but the conversation ends in a conspiracy against the public, or in some contrivance to raise prices."[224] Smith's reason for mentioning such a tendency, which has not lessened in our own day, was not to excuse it; indeed, Smith was a staunch advocate and defender of the small entrepreneur.

Meanwhile, we have been conditioned to believe that the economy must advance according to the dubious dictates of the "invisible hand" of the "free market." Yet the only thing really "invisible" about globalization is what transpires behind the closed doors of corporate boardrooms, far beyond the visible hand of due democratic process. Indeed, the frequency of corporate crimes increases in direct proportion to the number of closed-door meetings that take place. Obviously, the only thing truly "free" about the "free market" is the gratuitous economic handouts awarded to big business in good times and in bad, in sickness and in health. What has transpired from this ridiculous situation is no laughing matter: The modern corporation has emerged as the new imperial threat that, under a similar threat of tyranny long ago, forced our ancestors to flee the Old World. It would be no exaggeration to say that the despotism of Old World inequality has come full circle in the New World today. The tragedy, however, is that there are no more "New Worlds" to escape to.

The American rugged individual is becoming increasingly irrelevant by the spread of secretive organizations that provide the

---

224 Adam Smith, *An Inquiry into the Nature and Causes of the Wealth of Nations* (New York: Modern Library, 1937), 128.

goods, yet deny the necessities, which are, namely, democracy and autonomy. The international stage is big enough to host only a privileged number of transnational corporations; we the people need not apply. These business entities, in addition to their representation in the halls of American politics, enjoy top-shelf representation from a host of supranational organizations. "The 'global financial architecture' is a phrase that encompasses pretty much all of the acronyms we love to hate: the IMF, the OECD, the WTO, the Gs (7, 8, 10, 20), the FSF, FATF, the IBRD, the EBRD, the ADB, AFDB, the IDB, IFC, ECLAC," the *Financial Times* summarized. "There is no country so insignificant that it does not belong to at least half-a-dozen. And there isn't a bureaucrat from Conakry to Punto Arenas who doesn't dream of joining the gravy train."[225]

Clearly, corporate power makes the specter of an oppressive *political* regime—always the greatest fear of our forefathers due to their bloody experience with the Old World—seem greatly exaggerated in hindsight. Indeed, our greatest challenge today involves oppressive *economic* regimes, as opposed to oppression of a religious or political type. "Political dynasties have disappeared," Russell rightly warned, "but economic dynasties survive."[226]

GLOBALIZATION'S CRACKED FOUNDATION

Today, corporate representation rests with those mighty institutions that have been steadily evolving outside of legitimate, democratic procedure since the Bretton Woods Commission following World War II.[227] The best known is the pyramidal triumvirate of the World Trade Organization, International Monetary Fund, and the World Bank, now working assiduously to forge a

---

225 Andrew Hilton, "Body Count," *Financial World*, November 2008, 9.
226 Russell, *History of Western Philosophy*, 567.
227 "The Bretton Woods Commission's proposal represented the establishment's idea of an interim step toward the vision of eventual 'one world' governance....The IMF would be authorized to discipline governments in the advanced economies, more or less as it already does with the poorer developing nations." William Greider, *One World, Ready or Not* (New York: Simon & Schuster), 1997, 256.

one-world financial system.[228] These institutions, it was believed, would establish some degree of fairness and opportunity into the global economic paradigm, thus precluding any future martial passions (i.e., war) on the part of a desperate people. Ironically, despite such an ambitious program on behalf of personal freedom, liberty, and peace, much of the chaos of our times stems from the profound lack of democracy in these omnipotent financial organizations.[229]

The IMF and World Bank largely serve as behind-the-scenes advocates for corporate power and are essentially responsible for getting indebted nations to rewrite their social contracts in order to qualify for emergency loan packages. That these earth-shattering initiatives are being secretly approved behind closed doors, and without any representation by and for the people, makes a complete mockery of democratic theory. "The IMF is a public institution, established with money provided by taxpayers around the world," writes Joseph Stiglitz in *Globalization and Its Discontents.* "This is important to remember because it does not report directly to either the citizens who finance it or those whose lives it effects."[230] The conclusion that Stiglitz arrives at should be of great concern to everyone, considering that it was the rallying call for America's greatest historical upheaval: "The current system run by the IMF is one of taxation without representation."

---

228 Bruce Rich, director of the international program at Environmental Defense, wrote recently of another largely overlooked segment of the global economy known as ECAs (export credit agencies). "Much like the WTO, ECAs have a single-issue agenda: trade above all. By helping national champions conquer export markets, they pursue what is in essence a mercantilist strategy. Their strategy contradicts the advocates of economic globalization, who promise benefits for all involved, including the poor and the environment. The frictionless global economy is as much an ideological Utopia as the other great economic folly of the 20th century, communism." ("Trading in Dubious Practices," *Financial Times,* February 24, 2000.) Another less-mentioned "rich man's club"—the European Round Table (ERT), whose headquarters is hidden away on a side street in Brussels—represents forty-six European corporations with a combined net worth of almost $1 trillion, as well as a workforce of approximately five million people.

229 There is yet another layer of secrecy in the international economic structure, which could best be illustrated by the Bilderberg Group, a gathering of business and political elite who meet annually behind closed doors. The content of these events are never provided in-depth coverage by the mainstream media.

230 Joseph Stiglitz, *Globalization and Its Discontents* (London: Penguin Books, 2002), 12, 20.

Considering the extensive support that corporations receive from these powerful international organizations, it should be no surprise that only the largest business entities are capable of withstanding the disruptive winds of upheaval and change. Indeed, like vultures, they swoop down after the disaster and feed off the carrion. For the rest of the corporate global village, we are now obliged to follow the brutal law of the jungle: every man for himself. We do not have international organizations speaking out on our behalf, or bankrolling our business projects, or bailing out our families in days of crisis. We get "cash for clunkers" and are told to carry on. Because of their intense partnership with our government representatives, the individuals who need representation the least—the transnational corporations—are getting the most. This was not how the economic gurus sold globalization to the world.

The proponents of globalization promised that the consumers, employees, and citizens would be the primary benefactors from an open and globalized economy. Free and unregulated borders, they said, would be a blessing in the form of more and better jobs, combined with lower prices. The North American Free Trade Agreement (NAFTA) and the General Agreement on Tariffs and Trade (GATT), for example, would provide unlimited opportunities for consumers and the labor force. In the midst of the euphoria, as even the seemingly indestructible Soviet Union quietly crumpled before the ideology of corporate liberalism and free markets, some went so far as to proclaim "the end of history." The reality, however, has been much different. It may be closer to the truth if we summed up our modern situation as "the end of dignity."

Ellen Frank, professor of economics at Emmanuel College, puts to rest the myth of "benevolent globalization" with the following statement: "Globalized trade and production coincide with greater inequality both within and between countries. The reasons for this are complex—globalization weakens unions, strengthens multinationals, and increases competition and insecurity all around."[231] As long as our political leaders continue to support such a one-sided global strategy, America's rugged individual will

---

231 *Dollars and Sense:* http://www.dollarsandsense.org/archives/2003/0103dollar.html

fall under the truck of globalization and runaway corporate power. But instead of rethinking our economic system and substituting it with something that is sustainable both to man and his environment, we continue to talk about useless "reform" schemes.

It is important to remember that economic "reform" applies only to the economy as such; the financial institutions are primarily concerned about how to break down economic walls between people and cultures. What follows afterward for the workforce—slashed wages, lost jobs, and increased corporate power—is of only secondary consideration to the architects of the global economy. The ongoing reforms are designed to promote corporate power in the belief that the people will get pulled along in the process. This is failing to happen in spectacular fashion, and that is exactly why the people need to gain some control over their political process.

The leaders of the global financial organizations continue to be [s]elected through secret ballots, while meetings are held behind heavy doors beyond public scrutiny. Even the wicked castor oil reforms prescribed to ailing and healthy economies alike are never disclosed for public consideration and due debate. Only after the damage is done—and there has been unspeakable damage—are the crimes prattled about in the media. This handwringing exercise after the fact we somehow call democracy.

"The IMF and the World Bank promote markets but are interested only prudentially if at all in promoting democracy," writes one noted critic of Western-style globalization. "Indeed, they have shown themselves willing to sacrifice civic equilibrium and social equality for purely economic goals....They impose on fragile new would-be democracies economic crash plans that, while they suit the investment strategies of their member nations (and, more important, their member banks), also guarantee popular resentment."[232]

Meanwhile, even global leaders are increasingly "technocrats," chosen more for their loyalty to the financiers and central bankers. "The most powerful leader in Europe may be Mario Draghi, president of the European Central Bank, who was appointed by elected

232 B. Barber, 221.

officials but cannot be fired and is independent of political control," reported the *New York Times.* "Meanwhile, Greece and Italy are led by unelected technocrats whose selections were strongly influenced by Germany."[233] In 2009, Time magazine named Ben Bernanke person of the year for doing little more than handing out trillions of unaccounted dollars around the planet.

Today, transparency into the inner sanctum of the corporate and political worlds exists for an elite minority who believe that it is their sole right to speak for the good of society. Democrats need not apply. Due to the extreme precedence that the economy has taken in modern life, the economists seem to believe that the perplexities of long-term economic and social planning (no longer just a *soviet* event, it seems) should remain beyond the pale of democratic values; society will somehow be rewarded in the long-term for their lofty decisions. This narrow approach to the question of development on a global scale is a monstrous violation of democratic procedure. Given mankind's inherent selfishness, it is critical that the citizens of the world possess the guarantee of democratic representation within the tumultuous domain of economics. The application of democracy in the political realm is not enough to prevent abuses of power in the economic realm.

But getting a fair hearing on the free market is next to impossible since it was precisely the "free market" that devoured the free media. The conservative press—now practically mainstream throughout small-town America as most competitive voices were bought out many years ago—has spent many years characterizing regulation, taxation, and public-owned utilities as natural opponents of freedom, democracy, and most important, of course, capitalism. An individual who even breathes the words *regulation, higher taxes,* or *public assistance* is immediately branded a communist. Yet despite the partisan rhetoric, it remains the people who must shovel out the most in taxes to bail out "our" politicians' corporate clients, at the expense of guaranteed pension plans, health

---

233 Jack Ewing, *Across the World, Leaders Brace for Discontent and Upheaval,"* *New York Times,* January 25, 2012.

care, and Social Security. In the words of one wit: What we have today is socialism for the rich, and capitalism for everyone else.

In other words, democracy is failing to deliver the promised goods to the global village. Democratic theory sounds very logical on paper, which is what gives it such global appeal. Few can argue with its inner message, which is essentially freedom and equality for all. In order to bring about an egalitarian paradise inside our highly popu-lated societies, men and women are elected to stand and deliver on behalf of the people.[234] Unlike the case with ancient Athens, the very birthplace of democracy, we cannot reasonably expect all citizens to have a chance to speak their mind. These elected officials serve as the fulcrum point, the very axis upon which the heavy wheel of democracy turns. Thus, in a pluralistic society, the myriad needs and wants of the "general will" will be translated into reality by our rep-resentatives. But as more and more people are beginning to under-stand, achieving political fairness in these modern hard times is far more complicated than suggested in a university textbook.

The very nature of our sociopolitical system, dependent as it is on incessant change, guarantees that every tomorrow will be radically different from today. We are all passengers on the tech-nological juggernaut, and the emergency brakes stopped working many years ago. Such a turbulent climate demands that our politi-cal institutions be prepared to guide society through this veritable jungle of hidden unknowns. Thus far, however, in the face of take-no-prisoner globalization, democratic representation is utterly failing the people. Although we are granted a limited number of representatives to defend our interests, it is the "special" corpo-rate interests that receive the lion's share of government represen-tation due to their sheer economic clout. Corporate power now dominates not only globalization, but the political game as well.

Naturally, as if with everything, there are very real limitations to how much political representation any one government can pro-

---

234 Long before corporate power had infected the world of politics, Plato had observed that, "Those who are too smart to engage in politics are punished by being governed by those who are dumber;" centuries later, Thomas Jefferson voiced his own less-than-glowing estimation of the politician: "Whenever a man has cast a longing eye on offices, a rotten-ness begins in his conduct."

vide to its people; democratic representation is a limited resource and therefore cannot be squandered recklessly.[235] Given the well-known "ignorance and incompetence" of politicians—the "special curse of democracies" that Plato complained about in the *Republic*—the last thing our leaders need is another source of distraction.[236] We ignore at our own peril James Madison's oft-repeated observation that "Democracies...have in general been as short in their lives as they have been violent in their deaths."

MEDIA MANIPULATION & CONTROL

There is a good reason most people have no clue as to what is happening inside their proclaimed democracy: The spoken word is corporate-owned. This is the most disturbing problem for intelligent men to contemplate. While it remains no difficult thing to condemn excessive physical force through state-subsidized brutality (even a dog comprehends violence, after all), it remains a great problem demonstrating to the average citizen that an altogether different violence is being committed through the written—and unwritten—word. And when we speak of words, we must also speak of psychology, a conditioned state of mind—the mental effects words ingrain into the consciousness and subconsciousness of the highly malleable audience. "Power is always more secure when co-optive, covert, and manipulative than when nakedly brutish," writes Michael Parenti. "The support elicited through the control of minds is more durable than the support extracted at the point of a bayonet."[237]

Today, more than ever, most citizens receive their impressions of the world through the eyes of other men. Every day, a handful of news agencies deliver a carefully scripted version of reality (a

---

235   In June 2005, the *Washington Post* reported "the number of registered lobbyists in Washington has more than doubled since 2000 to more than 34,750 while the amount the lobbyists charge their new clients has increased by as much as 100 percent."

236   George H. Sabin, Thomas L. Thorson, *A History of Political Theory* (Indiana University, South Bend: Harcourt Brace College Publishers, 1973), 55.

237   Parenti, *Inventing Reality*, 24.

virtual reality) to a large percentage of the population. For these lethargic armchair "receivers," their understanding of the outside world—beyond the fringes of their work and home—exists in the form of television, newsprint and, to an ever-increasing degree, the Internet. "It's worse in the case of newspapers," states F. Scott Fitzgerald's main character, Amory Blaine, in his 1920 novel *This Side of Paradise*. "Any rich, unprogressive old party with that particularly grasping, acquisitive form of mentality known as financial genius can own a paper that is the intellectual meat and drink of thousands of tired, hurried men, men too involved in the business of modern living to swallow anything but pre-digested food."

The controversial linguist Noam Chomsky[238] outlined the *raison d'être* of the media through his controversial Propaganda Model: "It is the societal purpose served by state education as conceived by James Mill in the early days of the establishment of this system: to 'train the minds of the people to a virtuous attachment to their government,' as well as 'protecting privilege from the threat of public understanding and participation."[239] This system is perpetuated by a pattern of artistic duplicity and deception from the various available media that have a bad habit of showing a more discerning eye for the tyranny existing in other lands. Indeed, propaganda is becoming increasingly a question of what is *not* shown, as opposed to what is. "Much of what passes for journalism," argues Benjamin Barber, "is in fact mere titillation, dressed-up gossip, or polite prejudice. The media have abandoned civil society for the greater profits of the private sector."[240]

There are varying degrees of acceptability associated with each medium, and not everybody, of course, chooses the absolute "lowest frequency," that is, the most depraved selection of options available. But it is, generally and historically speaking, in the very

---

238 Many academics and, of course, members of the media, criticize Noam Chomsky for "speaking out of his field of specialty" when commenting on the media and American culture in general. However, as a linguist, Chomsky is probably more qualified than anybody to present his social views. As Caesar reminded his people: "This state is nothing more than a *word*."

239 Milan Rai, *Chomsky's Politics* (London: Verso, 1995), 22. This passage is quoted from Chomsky's book *Necessary Illusions: Thought Control in Democratic Societies*, 1989.

240 Barber, 286–7.

nature of man to amuse himself with less than exemplary entertainment. The Internet is the perfect example. Heralded by some
overly enthusiastic writers as the savior of democracy (the so-called
"electronic town hall," or "virtual demos"), it is being discredited
on that very pretext today by its progenitors.[241] It is turning into
an electronic magazine rack of eternal choices and temptations,
none of which truly serves to promote the condition of our democratic institutions.

Flowing from these diverse "news sources" is a mighty river of
poisoned messages, and the contamination occurs directly at the
spring. Here, the polluted source is once again corporate power.
They would argue innocence due to Internet capabilities, a free
press, democracy, and so forth. However, public enlightenment
must precede all formal debate. Meanwhile, only the supercorporations have the luxury to flood the markets with their mass
media, as well as afford the exorbitant advertising that they sell to
other like-minded corporations. Due to an ineffective educational
system, combined with a fatuous entertainment culture, people
have become too dumbed down to challenge what they hear, and
don't hear, courtesy of the corporate news. Therefore, except in
exceedingly rare, irrelevant cases, corporate interests feed the
populace the messages they want. Naturally, these messages never
seriously challenge the status quo. It would be foolish to expect a
fair debate concerning corporate labor issues or responsible environmental programs, for example, from the mouth of the corporate-owned media. Better to distract viewers with nonessential,
sensational stories.

David C. Korten, reflecting on the condition of the Western media, wrote: "Those who bear the costs of the system's

---

241   In two of the most extensive reports on the effects of the Internet, and computer use
in general, researchers at both Carnegie Mellon University and Stanford University, in
separate studies, concluded that prolonged use of this technology is leading to a more with-
drawn society. Norman Nie, the principal investigator for this study at Stanford, summed
up their experiment by concluding: "The more hours that people use the internet, the less
time they spend with real human beings." He is primarily concerned about the implications
for many people remaining "home, alone and anonymous." While in the 1998 study at
CMU, researchers found that Internet users experienced much higher levels of depression
and loneliness.

dysfunction have been stripped of decision-making power and are held in a state of confusion regarding the cause of their distress by corporate-dominated media that incessantly bombard them with interpretations of the resulting crisis based on the perceptions of the power holders. An active propaganda machinery controlled by the world's largest corporations constantly reassures us that consumerism is the path to happiness, governmental restraint of market excess is the cause of our distress, and economic globalization is both a historical inevitability and a boon to the human species. In fact, these are all myths propagated to justify profligate greed and mask the extent to which the global transformation of human institutions is a consequence of the sophisticated, well-funded, and intentional interventions of a small elite whose money enables them to live in a world of illusion apart from the rest of humanity."[242]

In brief, it should surprise nobody that it is not, nor ever will be, in the interests of the media, in its present form, to document the gross failures of our corporate-controlled society. The very extent of corporate power itself in Western society will not even be admitted to; that would be the equivalent of the vampire trying to find his reflection in the mirror. The corporate media provide a very limited and elitist forum for social debate, and they position themselves high above any and all questions concerning the very legitimacy of their existence.

"Media corporations are still corporations," as Milan Rai has stressed. "It would be surprising if they worked to undermine corporate interests."[243] And so we as a nation remain largely in the dark when it comes to grasping the truth of our plight and fight against corporate power.

---

242 David C. Korten, *When Corporations Rule the World* (New York: Kumarian Press, 1995), 12.
243 Rai, *Chomsky's Politics*, 23.

CHAPTER VII
The Decline and
Death of the American Empire

"I hope that we shall crush in its birth the moneyed corporations, which dare already to challenge our government to a trial of strength, and bid defiance to the laws of our country."

—THOMAS JEFFERSON

"Life's closest analogy to the...corporation is cancer. We get cancer when a genetic defect causes a cell to forget it is part of a larger whole and seeks its own unlimited growth without regard to the consequences."

—DAVID KORTEN

Up to this point, we have seen how corporate power has invaded the public realm and cast aside the main character on the American stage, which is not some bloodless corporation that can be bought and sold on the stock market, but rather the very human rugged individual. This usurpation has affected every area of our lives and, as we will now argue, profoundly altered the nation's moral landscape. As history has shown, no country can survive the destruction of its moral and spiritual foundation. From the increasingly degraded forms of entertainment, to how the military is ignoring international law in foreign lands, there is compelling evidence that something more than a change of attitude and behavior brought about by modernity is at play.[244] The intrusion of corporate power in every aspect our life is largely responsible for America's moral decline, which is merely a prelude to far greater problems.

Due to a series of devastating Supreme Court decisions, the corporate beast of burden, now blessed with "personhood," as well as the power to finance political campaigns, has been unleashed on an unsuspecting public. Yet this "person" never goes to jail or suffers the brunt of an economic crisis, which is no surprise since corporations pay more to lobby members of Congress than they do in taxes. In fact, many of these corporate persons excuse themselves from even paying any taxes at all. Obviously, the American people cannot compete against these economic powerhouses, where political and economic abuses of power have been practically institutionalized at the commanding heights.

Meanwhile, any attempt to assemble and protest against this behavior is met with extreme police force, which practically makes the Second Amendment a toothless statement. Gun ownership, which was designed to protect against such tyranny, is no longer the great equalizer the US Constitution expected it to be. At the same time, the mainstream media—the so-called Fourth Estate that would rigorously work on behalf of truth and justice—have become a corporate-owned asset, defending business interests simply because the media are a business interest. As a result of this treachery, democracy has been sold out like another commodity, while our representatives in government are slavishly devoted to

---

244 According to the US Bureau of Justice Statistics' most recent report, incidences of violent crime jumped 18 percent in 2011, while property crimes were up 11 percent. Household burglaries rose 14 percent, and the number of thefts jumped by 10 percent. Bureau of Justice web page: bjs.ojp.usdoj.gov/index.cfm?ty=tp&tid=31.

their corporate paymasters. What recourse do we have when our voice has been silenced; when protest is strangled; when fear and intimidation rule the day? Thomas Paine would have certainly agreed: "These are times that try men's souls."

Case in point: the American war machine. This government-subsidized Frankenstein's monster, better known as the military-industrial complex, shows that the American government has no problem socializing the corporate defense sector. The price tag for the Pentagon's military hardware, its international network of military bases, and its disastrous overseas adventures has already surpassed the trillion-dollar-per-year mark. Nobody, however, is demanding "austerity measures" against this out-of-control death machine. The real problem with the US military, however, is more profound and speaks volumes about the consequences of extreme corporate power. We are talking about the behavior of the troops. Human rights abuses from Guantanamo Bay to Abu Ghraib are revealing a dark side of the American character never before seen in the history of warfare.

Although the United States has been involved over the years in many overseas conflicts, most notably in World War II and Vietnam, the conduct exhibited by our soldiers in the so-called War on Terror has been nothing less than appalling. In fact, it has even been called sadistic. That painful indictment came from our closest and most valuable foreign ally, the United Kingdom. What prompted the remark was the case of Ethiopian-born Binyam Mohamed, who was granted refugee status in the UK in 1994. In 2002, Mohamed was arrested in Pakistan over a visa technicality and duly handed over to US military officials. This was the start of a seven-year nightmare for Mr. Mohamed, who was tortured in Morocco by interrogators before being sent to the Guantanamo Bay detention center, where he was held without any charges brought against him until his release in February 2009.

Once back in the UK, Binyam Mohamed sought legal redress for major grievances. In a surprise ruling, the UK court ruled that US intelligence information involving this specific case must be released into the public domain. Although London and Washington have a long history of intelligence-sharing, the UK Court of Appeal, despite howls of protest from US officials, released[245] the following redacted information in the case describing Mohamed's brutal treatment at the hands of his American captors:

v. Binyam Mohamed (BM) had been intentionally subjected to sleep deprivation. The effects of the sleep deprivation were carefully observed.

vi. It was reported that combined with sleep deprivation, threats and inducements were made on him. His fears of being removed from United States custody and "disappearing" were played upon.

vii. It was reported that the stress brought about by these deliberate tactics was increased by him being shackled in his interviews.

viii. It was clear…he was being kept under self-harm [suicide] observation, that the interviews were having a marked effect upon him and causing him significant mental stress and suffering.

The UK court concluded by stating, "Although it is not necessary for us to categorize the treatment reported, it could readily be contended to be at the very least cruel, inhuman and degrading treatment by the United States authorities." Admittedly, war is a nasty business, and there will always be instances of cruelty and the killing of innocents so long as men choose to resolve their differences with bombs and bloodshed. Nevertheless, when and how did America turn into a nation that exposes its prisoners of war to "cruel, inhuman and degrading" treatment?

But the Binyam Mohamed case was just the tip of the iceberg as far as US military abuses were concerned. In a previous chapter, we touched upon the subject of black hole sites in Eastern Europe, where US officials and their allies were able to carry out "legal" interrogations of suspects—delivered to these secret facilities in cooperation with various European governments—without fear-

---

245 Information from UK Foreign & Commonwealth Office website: www.fco.gov.uk.

ing public scrutiny. Eventually, however, the truth leaked into the public domain thanks to the release of a single photograph—postmarked Guantanamo Bay—that convinced many people that our nation had completely hit the rails in terms of moral and spiritual behavior. The photo, seen by the entire world, shows a detainee donning bright-orange prison garb, kneeling in the sand, hands and feet bound, inside a razor-wire enclosure. Those extraordinary precautions, however, were apparently not quite enough to quell our sadistic appetites.

The US military also found it necessary to force the detainees, many of them innocent of the charges against them, to wear "sensory-deprivation" gear, including earmuffs, face masks, and blindfolds. Keep in mind that the prisoners are on an island inside a military enclosure, surrounded by gun-toting soldiers not to mention sharks, and are denied the ability to even inhale air in the sweltering Caribbean heat. Is there any logical way to explain this vicious brutality? After all, the United States is the world's leader in state-of-the-art, inescapable "supermax" prison systems, which house some 500,000 of the world's most dangerous inmates. Not even Houdini himself could get out of these complexes. Thus, to say that we were forced to take these medieval-style precautions against these individuals—who are, after all, mere mortals—is ridiculous, inexcusable, and a grievous blow to our national reputation.

And that is only what we know from the available photographs. What sort of nocturnal nightmares these individuals experienced behind closed doors is another matter, although pieces of the puzzle are slowly emerging. One thing that we do know is that American interrogators used "waterboarding" against two members of al-Qaeda a total of 266 times. Waterboarding is an interrogation technique that gives the subject the overwhelming sensation of being drowned. (Christopher Hitchens, the late writer and social critic who doubted the severity of this "enhanced interrogation technique," subjected himself to waterboarding, but not before signing the following contract of indemnification: *"'Waterboarding' is a potentially dangerous activity on which the participant can receive serious and permanent (physical, emotional and psychological) injuries*

183

and even death, including injuries and death due to the respiratory and neurological systems of the body." Hitchens lasted no more than a few seconds before ending the experiment.)

According to a 2005 Justice Department legal memorandum, "the C.I.A. used waterboarding 183 times in March 2003 against Khalid Shaikh Mohammed,"[246] the alleged planner of the 9/11 terrorist attacks. Aside from the obvious questions concerning the humane treatment of prisoners, how reliable is the information obtained from Mr. Mohammed under such diabolical conditions? It is already known that the most willful individual will quickly confess to any crime if the torture is drawn out long enough.

Thus, in light of Khalid Shaikh Mohammed's inhumane treatment at the behest of our modern-day Inquisition, the American public has the right to hear this individual testify in person on the charges brought against him. The American people, who suffered three thousand deaths on 9/11, deserve to hear this man speak. That, of course, will never be allowed to happen. All of the detainees at Guantanamo Bay have been denied a civil (read: public) trial, which means the American people must accept the official story, embellished by a craven and corrupt media, that this individual, whose testimony has been given behind the steel doors of a military tribunal, is guilty of the charges brought against him under extreme duress. Thus, the American people will never truly feel closure on the events of 9/11.

But more to the point of our argument: As it turned out, this extremely disturbing treatment of prisoners of war was being imitated by the rank-and-file of the US military in extraordinarily different ways.

WELCOME TO ABU GHRAIB AND THE CORPORATE ZOMBIES

The horrors of Guantanamo Bay were not an isolated case of bad judgment. Across the ocean, and in a different war, detain-

---

246 Scott Shane, "Waterboarding Used 266 Times on 2 Suspects," *New York Times*, April 19, 2009.

ees held at the Abu Ghraib Confinement Facility in Iraq were also suffering vicious, sadistic treatment by their American captors. According to the Taguba Report,[247] which was commissioned by the US military to investigate and document the abuses, it was shown that between October and December 2003 "numerous incidents of sadistic, blatant, wanton criminal abuses were inflicted on several detainees."

HERE IS A LIST OF THE ABUSES REPORTED:

a. Punching, slapping, and kicking detainees; jumping on their naked feet;

b. Videotaping and photographing naked male and female detainees;

c. Forcibly arranging detainees in various sexually explicit positions for photographing;

d. Forcing detainees to remove their clothing and keeping them naked for several days at a time;

e. Forcing naked male detainees to wear women's underwear;

f. Forcing groups of male detainees to masturbate themselves while being photographed and videotaped;

g. Arranging naked male detainees in a pile and then jumping on them;

h. Positioning a naked detainee on a MRE box, with a sandbag on his head, and attaching wires to his fingers, toes, and penis to simulate electric torture;

i. Writing "I am a Rapest (sic)" on the leg of a detainee alleged to have forcibly raped a fellow fifteen-year-old fellow detainee, and then photographing him naked;

j. Placing a dog chain or strap around a naked detainee's neck and having a female soldier pose for a picture;

k. A male MP guard having sex with a female detainee;

---

247   The Taguba Report is available at www.npr.org/iraq/2004/prison_abuse_report.pdf.

l. Using military working dogs (without muzzles) to intimidate and frighten detainees, and in at least one case biting and severely injuring a detainee;

m. Taking photographs of dead Iraqi detainees.

For any person with their moral bearings still intact, it is very difficult to read the above description of abuses carried out by Americans without wondering what has gone wrong with our national psyche. This behavior, although carried out by a few military groups (the 372nd Military Police Company, 320th Military Police Battalion, 800th MP Brigade), and reported by US officials, nevertheless points to a deep national moral crisis. No level of aggression against the United States can justify such cruel and sadistic behavior; otherwise, we are no better than the enemy we are fighting. And as bad as things got in World War II, or Vietnam, it is difficult to imagine our GIs behaving in such a lewd and sadistic manner. In fact, the conduct indicates that the real battlefield facing most Americans is not overseas, but rather at home. The symptom of extreme corporate power in our lives, which represses the spirit and creative impulses of the individual, is creating something that I can only refer to as "corporate zombies;" individuals who have been nurtured from birth on a soul-destroying diet of corporate garbage and who now are void of all moral scruples. The fact that these individuals were brought to justice, however, serves as a reminder that not everybody has been victimized by this form of "zombyism." Nevertheless, corporate power and influence—which runs the gamut from television screening, to films, to products, to taking over private proprietorship—has clearly had an effect on the American psyche, and not in a positive way.

Here is what one commentator had to say regarding the sadistic behavior of US troops in the "War on Terror": "Posing with dead, tortured Muslims or their body parts is an all-too-common exercise in the military since 9/11 – whether in the Abu Ghraib torture dungeon, the urban kill zones of Iraq, or the arid plains of blood-soaked Afghanistan. But it's not just smiling and flashing a thumbs up for the camera, it's killing civilians… They also took photos of their gruesome escapades."[248]

I will leave it up to the reader to decide whether this type of behavior is normal among troops in every war in every age, or if a disturbing number of soldiers, born and bred on a diet of base corporate messages, are acting no better than our worst enemy. After all, can we really believe that a dumbed-down, violence-drenched entertainment industrial complex will not eventually produce some sort of deleterious affect on the 'consumer'? A corporate zombie if you will?

Fortunately, there is still a large number of exceptional American soldiers serving in the military; otherwise such atrocities would never have come to light in the first place. Indeed, it was whistleblowers inside of the Army that broke these stories. Nevertheless, it is the increasing frequency of this inhumane trend that must concern and disturb us, especially since there may come a day when our government, in the event of wide scale public unrest (triggered by economic collapse, environmental collapse, food shortages?), calls upon the military to "maintain order." Will the majority of troops heed the call, or will they honor the Constitution? The possibility of such a thing occurring increased greatly on December 31, 2011, when President Obama signed the National Defense Authorization Act (NDAA), codifying indefinite military detention without charge or trial into law for the first time in US history.

PRIVATE MILITARY CORPORATIONS—IT WAS ONLY A MATTER OF TIME

Yet another reason for the breakdown of discipline and conduct on the part of the American soldier is that the US military is increasingly made up of mercenary forces, otherwise known as private military corporations (PMCs). PMCs enjoy an estimated $100 billion in global business annually, with much of the money going

---

248 John Glaser, "Posing with the Dead, Dehumanizing the Enemy," Antiwar.com, April 18, 2012.

to Fortune 500 firms such as Halliburton, Lockheed Martin, and Raytheon. These martial powers being handed over to defense corporations, which have a direct financial interest in dragging out conflicts for as long as possible, should not surprise anybody. Given the extreme political powers corporations have achieved, it stands to reason that they would eventually have standing armies at their command.

In an academic paper focusing on the use of PMCs in modern conflicts, a connection is made between the use of corporate armies and the breakdown of governance and accountability in the military: "It is often implicitly or explicitly assumed that it is business interests—rather than international and national law—that govern the use and conduct of PMCs. There is, in this context, good reason to be concerned about leaving issues of peace and war, life and death, to purely market mechanisms. It would be naive, of course, to assume that traditional armed forces are necessarily virtuous and private armies inherently harmful to public interests. But the fact that profit-driven interests play a role in conflict does complicate control, transparency, and accountability issues."[249] Indeed, it is not difficult to imagine these profit-driven soldiers of fortune provoking the situation where they are stationed in order to extend their lucrative contracts. War, after all, is a business.

If these postmodern corporate times have taught us anything, it is that crime on an organized, supranational level is never punished. In fact, more often than not it is rewarded. That was the most disturbing aspect about the human rights abuses documented at Abu Ghraib and Guantanamo Bay. In this post-9/11 world, where the mere utterance of the word "terrorism" exonerates any misdeed and misjudgment, the people directly responsible for America's fall from grace were in many cases promoted. As Seymour Hersh, veteran journalist, concluded: "Despite Abu Ghraib and Guantanamo—not to mention Iraq and the failure of intelligence—and the various roles they played in what went

---

249 Simon Chesterman and Chia Lehnardt, "From Mercenaries to Market: The Rise and Regulation of Private Military Companies," *New York University Public Law and Legal Theory Working Papers.* Paper 55. July 20, 2007.

wrong, (Donald) Rumsfeld kept his job; (Condoleezza) Rice was promoted to secretary of state; Alberto Gonzales, who commissioned the memos justifying torture, became attorney general; deputy secretary of defence Paul Wolfowitz was nominated to the presidency of the World Bank; and Stephen Cambone, undersecretary of defense for intelligence and one of those most directly involved in the policies of prisoners, was still one of Rumsfeld's closest confidants."[250]

Whenever there is a connection between government and corporate power, crime and corruption can be expected to run rampant. Like the bankers and financiers who wrecked the global economy and woke up the next day to bailout checks and Christmas bonuses, our military personnel—who increasingly consist of corporate mercenaries—are exempt from facing the consequences of their actions. In September 2007, for example, seventeen innocent civilians were gunned down by Blackwater USA guards in Baghdad's Nusour Square. The unprovoked attack also left dozens wounded. One year later, the United States charged the five Blackwater guards with fourteen counts of manslaughter and twenty counts of attempted manslaughter. But on December 31, 2009, a US judge dismissed all of the charges, and the perpetrators walked free. So what course of action did Blackwater USA take following this public relations fiasco? It changed its corporate logo, of course.

"Founded by former Navy SEAL Erik Prince, the original Blackwater cultivated a special-operations mystique," reported the *Wall Street Journal*. "But it was tarnished by a string of high-profile incidents, including a deadly 2007 shootout in Iraq that ultimately led to its reorganization and rebranding as Xe Services."[251] Today, the Virginia-based company is now known as Academi following its latest makeover. Once a brand name has been tarnished by an atrocity, corporate executives can simply purchase a new logo and all is forgotten.

---

250 Seymour M. Hersh, "Abu Ghraib," *Znet*, May 23, 2005.
251 Nathan Hodge, "Company Once Known as Blackwater Ditches XE for Yet Another New Name," *Wall Street Journal*, December 12, 2011.

No amount of corporate rebranding, however, can change a simple fact about this and other similar organizations: They are mercenary outfits operating in war zones with practical immunity.

The United Nations issued a report in October 2007 condemning the increasingly frequent use of mercenary groups by the United States. "The trend toward outsourcing and privatizing various military functions by a number of member states in the past 10 years has resulted in the mushrooming of private military and security companies," the panel wrote in a report that was presented to the UN General Assembly in November 2007. The "tremendous increase" in the number of such private military companies, including those working alongside the State Department and Defense Department, has occurred in Afghanistan and Iraq, the report stated. The United States, however, which never signed a 1989 UN treaty making it illegal for one country to hire foreign soldiers for use in a third, rejected the findings of the report. Apparently, being a global superpower carries certain privileges.

Meanwhile, it is the United States that must shoulder the blame for this outrageous conduct. "The idea that the United States government should accept liability for the unprovoked criminal manslaughter of seventeen innocent Iraqis by Blackwater mercenaries, and place it on the back of taxpayers, is corporate animism run amok," the politician and public activist Ralph Nader was quoted as saying in an article by the *Nation*. "If Blackwater wants to be treated like a person, then its latest mutation…should be prosecuted, convicted and given the equivalent penalty of corporate capital punishment by revoking its charter and terminating its corporate operations."[252]

Superpower status notwithstanding, the sharp increase in the use of PMCs has created a moral vacuum—a lawless no-man's land in the middle of conflicts—where the United States can turn a blind eye to the Geneva Convention as corporate mercenaries carry out their shadowy operations with zero democratic oversight. "Private military corporations become a way to distance themselves and create what we used to call 'plausible deniability,'"

---

[252] Jeremy Scahill, "Making Sense of the Blackwater Connection," *Nation*, August 2009.

Daniel Nelson, a former professor of civil-military relations at the Marshall European Center for Security Studies, told *Mother Jones.* "It's disastrous for democracy."[253]

Indeed, the balancing act of corporations acting with immunity on the battlefield, as the United States trumpets "democracy building," cannot continue forever. The idea takes the entire notion of "corporate personhood" to its most obscene degree and severely disrupts America's foreign policy. It makes a farce of American military objectives in foreign lands, not to mention permits corporations to manipulate global hotspots for private gain.

Most disturbing, however, is that America's military conduct abroad speaks volumes about what is happening to the American character, influenced as it is by corporate power run amok. When the greatest "personality" on the global stage, that is, the US corporation, is able to behave without scruples, without morals, without punishment, then it is only a matter of time before that same degenerate code of conduct is imitated by those struggling underneath the jackboot—the American people.

Meanwhile, it is not just in the business of war that America's true colors are being exposed; America's fall from spiritual grace is also captured in the reckless approach to life and the natural world.

CORPORATIONS VERSUS NATURE

Since at least the eighteenth century and severely underestimating his ability for having an impact on the planet, man has been waging a relentless war against nature.[254] Armed with the sophisticated tools of the laboratory, science has set out on a great safari hunt to extract all of nature's intimate secrets. Today, those

---

253 Barry Yeoman, "Soldiers of Good Fortune," *Mother Jones*, May/June 2003.
254 Writing on the need to transform scientific inquiry in his famous *Novum Organum*, Francis Bacon boldly stated: "We must put nature on the rack and compel her to bear witness, so that her well-guarded secrets may advance the material condition of science and humanity." He would probably be appalled if he could see how literally we have interpreted his metaphorical advice.

secrets—from the microscopic world to the vast expanse of the solar system—are not being categorized for the purpose of advancing knowledge, or even the condition of life, but for advancing the power and profits of the multinational corporations. The consequences from such a narrow strategy are not only the demise and irreversible destruction of the natural world, but irreparable damage to the physical and spiritual condition of mankind. Out of nature man was born, and within nature man must continue to live. Yet we ignore at grave risk to our very species this common sense.

I will not be so bold as to speak on nature's behalf; it would be pure folly to suppose that nature needs a spokesperson. Nature will take care of itself, and it has done so many millions of years before man emerged upon the world stage. When our childish games have proved too burdensome for the intricate web of life to assimilate, we shall be relieved of our stay upon the planet and another page from the great book of evolution will be quietly turned. The planet has experienced great destruction before and, sad as the loss of species and habitats may be for the human conscience to contemplate, creative destruction is an essential part of her business plan.

If protecting nature is a fool's game, protecting our children and ourselves may be a bit more realistic. We are able to decide, through our natural intelligence, how we should conduct ourselves as guests during our brief stay both for the good of the planet and the good of all future living things. As it stands, however, the planet has simply become a carnival ground for the daily follies of capitalism, which is largely based upon the idea of acquiring ephemeral, short-lived consumption and entertainment at the expense of the natural world.[255] The definition of democracy itself has practically become one and the same as entertainment. As a result, we—as a living species that depends on a healthy Earth for its survival—have no moral understanding as to what exactly is at stake.

---

255 The Geneva-based World Conservation Union (IUCN), in its annual Red List, documented more than eighteen thousand species of animals and plants that are now at great risk of possible extinction.

At this point, there is no sense repeating statistics concerning the plight of the ecosystem. That will get us nowhere. We need to look deeper to truly fathom what the loss of nature means for the human spirit. For many of us, this will not be easy. The majority of humanity has been raised upon the unforgiving pavement of urban landscapes and isolated itself behind one form of computer-driven virtual reality. This has crushed all but the most sensitive souls and erased the poetry of life. At the same time, we have grown accustomed to an inordinate amount of comfort, ease, and ennui, while many people no longer come face-to-face with the natural world, nor even the fluctuating conditions of changing weather patterns.

The new religion is technology, where people genuflect before the promise of tangled wires and hardware inherent to our so-called Knowledge Age. The majority of our daily routine is spent staring at the glass barrier of a windshield, computer screen, or television, while communicating with friends and family has been largely reduced to some form of "social media." One of the most disturbing consequences of this mass dislocation is that the natural world has become distant, remote, and even irrelevant, we believe, from everyday experience. "Out of sight, out of mind," as the aphorism goes.

In short, poetry, not to mention the absolute spring of all artistic and educational pursuits, is fading away along with the endangered species, the lush rain forests and the majestic mountains. It cannot be denied that our detachment from the natural world is largely responsible for America's present moral and spiritual decline, and, vice versa, our ongoing moral decline is responsible for the deplorable state of nature. Many of us are able to sense our detachment from the natural world, yet we are helpless in restoring a real connection to the ultimate life source. Sherwood Anderson, in a letter to Waldo Frank in the 1920s, summarized this innate yearning and attachment that man once held with the natural world: "Is it not likely that when the country was new and men were often alone in the fields and the forest they got a sense of bigness outside themselves that has now in some way been lost....Mystery whispered in the grass, played in the branches of trees overhead, was caught up and blown across the American line in clouds of dust at evening on the prairies....I am old enough to remember tales that strengthen my belief in a deep semi-religious influence that was formerly at work among our people. The flavor of it hangs over the work of Mark Twain....I can remember old fellows in my hometown speaking feelingly of an evening spent on the big empty plains. It had taken the shrillness out of them. They had learned the trick of quiet."

The last line is worth repeating: *"The flavor of it hangs over the work of Mark Twain....I can remember old fellows in my hometown speaking feelingly of an evening spent on the big empty plains. It had taken the shrillness out of them. They had learned the trick of quiet."*

When man is left alone to ponder the vastness of the natural world, far removed from store-bought sensations, only then is it possible to speak about constructing a moral foundation for society. Yet the artificial, corporate world-inside-of-a-world is attempting to become the middleman between man and his natural world. Thus, we have become superdependent on corporate benevolence to provide us with all of our required provisions. And should our corporate overlords simply decide one day to close up shop and stop providing us with the basic necessities of life—food, clothing, and shelter, not to mention banks—the streets will explode in the worst scenes of panic and pandemonium ever seen. The potential consequences of our dependence is not lost on us; most Americans can comprehend how deeply dependent they have become on outside forces to provide for all of our needs. This creates an internal dread and apprehension in most people, although they may not understand the source of their discomfort. Superdependence on the benevolence of any outside entity—be it the state or corporate power—cuts across the grain of our true natures and compromises the essence of our rugged individualism. After all, man has been one with the natural world for many millennia before the arrival of our "modern age," and powerful feelings of attachment to the environment will never fade.

To better understand what is happening to the moral fabric of the American people with their detachment from the natural world, consider the words of Wallace Stegner, who spoke at the Sierra Club's Seventh Biennial Wilderness Conference in 1960: "It seems distinct to me that the distinct downturn in our literature from hope to bitterness took place almost at the precise time when the frontier officially came to an end, in 1890, and when the American way of life had begun to turn strongly urban and industrial. The more urban it has become, and the frantic with technological change, the sicker and more embittered our literature, and I believe our people, have become."

As Stegner, together with millions of other Americans inherently understand, every aspect of man's life is becoming urban, unnatural, and artificial. This is problematic for our survival within a finite biological system. The best example can be witnessed through our very food production. Although there have been real cultural advantages to relieving man from the great burden of cultivating his own food supply, we have seriously abused our capabilities. So dire is our plight as a species that the life of the autonomous farmer is looking increasingly like man's last hope for redemption on earth.

The question, then, is how to save man—not the environment—from "man-made activities." Human beings got along very well with the natural world—that is, until the decision was made to construct an iron economic matrix over the life-giving planet in order to enrich and empower a small number of corporations and their government representatives. These individuals are now enjoying the ultimate harvest at the expense of the moral and spiritual destruction of the planet. Physical destruction is secondary to the moral collapse of the human species. Genetically manipulated crops, corporate farming techniques, and dumping millions of tons of waste—much of it biodegradable—into sprawling garbage dumps dishonors every aspect of man's existence. It violently severs man from the circle of life, and makes him something of a detached tourist—like a space traveler to a distant planet. Once men and women are made a slave to the corporate system, as is now the case, they will not only lack the moral compass to steer away from the rocks of physical (that is, environmental) collapse, but will not have the freedom to do so even if they wanted.

The American people, and against their natures, became hyperdependent on corporate power without considering the consequences of that enslavement. And now that corporations provide us with everything under the sun, including the very information and news we need in order to make rational decisions, we are limited in our abilities to reconnect ourselves to the natural world. Indeed, many of us lack the elementary understanding of our situation to demand the change in the first place. Yet, at the same time, it is impossible to ignore the inner voice of freedom and independence that is practically a genetic trait of the American people.

Americans are experiencing an internal moral struggle: On the one hand, we are being bombarded with corporate-sponsored messages that our corporate-bought lifestyles is what we want; on the other hand, we are being pulled by the natural tendency inherent in every American to restore the connection with our "rugged individualism," which would require us to give up our corporate chains and reconnect—at least to some degree—with the natural world.

The corporate matrix does not permit for any sort of real freedom and independence of the entrepreneurial sort, which for many is the very definition of freedom, especially inside a capitalist society trumpeting itself as a democracy. The idea of freedom has been marketed and plastic-wrapped for us by corporate overlords and available in ten thousand different flavors. Yet the corporate world understands—much better than we do—that what makes man truly content, what gives him real peace of mind, is the knowledge that he is an independent player who does not require one million square feet of shopping space dropped into the middle of his community to be happy. Happiness, true inner, spiritual happiness, is not something that can be bought. Happiness of the moral type, otherwise known as contentment, comes from a man providing largely for himself. The secondary, store-bought sensations may complement life, but they can never serve as a means to an end.

Yet that is exactly where we now find ourselves: We as a nation have become so mesmerized by materialism, commercialism, and consumerism that we are severely damaging the planet in our endless hot pursuit. Although many are still in a state of denial on the subject, the majority of scientists—at least those who do not receive subsidies from the corporate world—concede that the natural world is suffering irreparable damage due to man-made (read: corporate) activities. Due to man-made globalization, which is a very recent phenomenon, the earth is now experiencing its most profound physical changes since the "the last global-scale critical transition, when 30% of Earth's surface went from being covered by glacial ice to being ice-free," according to a recent academic paper.[256]

The scientists in the abovementioned study pointed to human population growth and per-capita consumption as the leading cause for Earth's plight. The human population has almost quadrupled in the past century, while the most conservative estimates, according to the report, predict the planet's population will grow from its present value of 7 billion to 9 billion by 2045.

What does this unprecedented growth mean? Nobody knows for sure, but our inability to grapple with the issue suggests at the very least an internal moral collapse. All we can do is look at the current condition of the planet and recite numbing statistics: "As a result of human activities…biological change has now emerged," including the conversion of about "43% of Earth's land to agricultural or urban landscapes, with much of the remaining natural landscapes networked with roads." At the same time, "[R]apid climate change shows no signs of slowing." The study goes on to warn: "Climates found at present on 10–48% of the planet are projected to disappear within a century, and climates that contemporary organisms have never experienced are likely to cover 12–39% of Earth. The mean global temperature by 2070 (or possibly a few

---

256 Anthony D. Barnosky (lead researcher among a group of twenty-one other scientists), "Approaching a State Shift in Earth's Biosphere," *Nature*, June 2012.

decades earlier) will be higher than it has been since the human species evolved." In other words, nothing to be overly optimistic about. This data derives from rock-solid scientific research, conducted by individuals who have no personal stake (aside from their own survival) in the present corporate-dominated economic paradigm. Yet we casually shrug it off.

Despite the multitude of dire warnings from the scientific community, which is simply presenting the results of computer-generated scenarios, the people who control the flow of information—the corporate-owned media establishments—downplay and even ridicule these hugely important scientific findings. Such indifference in the face of potentially catastrophic environmental change was expressed by former US President George W. Bush. In an effort to explain why America, the world's biggest energy user, would not sign the Kyoto Protocol, a treaty to slash greenhouse gases, he said: "Kyoto would have wrecked our economy."[257] (Meanwhile, Bush's successor, Barack Obama, seems equally restrained from putting the brakes on economic consumption and destruction in the name of saving ourselves and the planet from imminent and monumental change). Bush's reasoning for doing nothing in the face of scientific facts perfectly summarizes America's plight, not only when it comes to restoring the natural environment, but for battling against corporate power. Think about it. If our leaders are willing to sacrifice the very health and even survival of the planet—the life-giving source behind all of our economic pursuits—for the sake of a robust earnings report, then how will they respond when they are forced to make a decision about democracy in the workplace? We already know that answer. It is clear that when the question of helping corporations to achieve their "personal happiness" (i.e., massive profits) arises, our leaders will always bend over backward to help. When the matter is the American citizen attempting to receive some semblance of justice and fair wages in this corporate-dominated society, well, good luck with that.

---

257 "Bush: Kyoto Treaty Would Have Hurt Economy," Associated Press, June 30, 2005.

CONCLUSION

As corporate power has come to dominate all facets of American life, democratic procedure has not kept pace. In fact, as the government continues to cosy up to corporate power, it has been practically destroyed. As this book has attempted to demonstrate, it is altogether impossible for the American people to compete against these economic monstrosities in the social, economic and political realms. This preponderance of excessive corporate power in every area of life is thought to be permissible by simply whistling the old, worn-out tune called "free market." The victim of this grand deception, of course, is the American people.

Here is something everybody must consider: All U.S. corporations and their top executives have benefited from the trillions of middle-class taxpayer dollars used to bailout the financial system. This is a heavy footnote that has been neglected in the debate over corporate power. We the American people empower the corporations not only with our labor but also with our purchasing power. Thus, corporations are social constructs underwritten by We the People! This means there should be no opportunity for these economic powerhouses to lend their financial support to any particular political program. Not only because such behavior is unconstitutional, but because we have the legal authority to deny them this outrageous privilege. Yet we continue to allow an infinitesimal minority to make a mockery of our democratic institutions. These individuals, some of whom we've mentioned in this work, do not speak on behalf of their employees or customers as our government representatives are paid to do. Indeed, if corporations work hard to silence their workers' voices at the workplace, they will certainly deny their voice in the halls of political power. It's time to call a spade a spade. The 'freedom of speech' now enjoyed by the corporate executive class (through their financial clout, which the American people contributed to) in our political process is totally out of proportion to their representational powers. Their participation in our democratic process is nothing less than treachery. Full stop.

None of this, of course, should be misconstrued as an argument against capitalism, as some will certainly attempt to argue. This is an argument against the ability of one powerful economic player to monopolize the social, cultural, and political sectors of American society for intense private gain. Such brazen, unchecked powers make a mockery of our democratic process, not to mention the constitutionally guaranteed "pursuit of happiness." However, thanks to a number of extremely dangerous Supreme Court rulings, which we have already discussed, American corporations are in their political ascendancy. They enjoy the supreme power of financing political campaigns without needing to disclose any information involving the transactions. At a time when we should be concerned with the way American workers are being treated inside the corporate universe, we are instead forced to consider how to extract corporations out of the democratic system.

The problem with extreme levels of corporate power, bad as it is, goes deeper than just a case of political disenfranchisement. Excessive corporate power has infiltrated into every corner of American life, to the point that it has gravely affected the overall condition of our morality and spirituality. This last chapter—citing as examples the extreme misbehavior of American soldiers in foreign wars, together with the destruction of the natural environment—spoke about the moral failings of the American people. That indictment was not easy to write. For most of my life I have believed that America was truly the beacon on the hill that shined the way for the rest of the world. Now I am not so sure. But I want my faith restored, as do many other Americans at this critical juncture in our nation's history.

The best way to restore the American Dream, and ensure that the United States remains true to itself, is to curb the powers of the corporation, which will never be content doing what it does best—making money. Clearly, these economic monstrosities have some sort of devilish desire to control the entire game. Such a thing can never be permitted to materialize inside a nation that prides itself on being a democracy. It is time to empower, once again, the most deserving character on the American stage, which is, and always will be, the American individual.

In closing, it would be wise to consider the words of John Quincy Adams, the sixth President of the United States, who understood how fragile the flower of democracy is: *"Democracy—while it lasts— is more bloody than either aristocracy or monarchy. Remember, democracy never lasts long. It soon wastes, exhausts, and murders itself. There is never a democracy that did not commit suicide."*[258]

In order to prove Mr. Adams wrong, as he would certainly want us to do, the American people must harness corporate power and reclaim their dominant role once again inside of this great nation.

---

258 In a letter to John Taylor, dated April 15th, 1814.

INDEX

Made in the USA
Columbia, SC
28 January 2021